YOUR PATH
TO
IMPACT THE WORLD

Samuel A. Liadi

Published by Gloripub
http://www.gloripub.com
Printed in the U.S.A
Your Path to Impact the World
Copyright © 2020 Samuel A. Liadi
All rights reserved solely by the author. The author guarantees all contents are original and do not infringe upon the legal rights of any other person or work. No part of this book may be reproduced in any form except for brief quotations in printed reviews, without the permission of the author.
Request for information should be addressed to:
Samuel Liadi at samliadi2013@gmail.com

ISBN-13: 9781735306506

Acknowledgments

Foremost, I would like to thank God Almighty, whom, through the Lord Jesus Christ, called me by His sovereign will to be a vessel of honor unto Him (2 Timothy 2:21), Thanks be to God who sent His Son to accomplish His salvific, justifying work on the cross and to Him who gave His Spirit that causes us to cry 'Abba Father,' to Him be the glory, honor and adoration forever and ever... Amen.

I especially acknowledge my late parents most especially, my beloved mother (Madam Sidikat Liadi nee Ashimolowo), who invested all to get me educated, raising me with discipline and morals. Love you, mom, I miss so much, continue to Rest in Peace Mom!

To my wife and my lovely children (Tomisin, Olaoluwa and Darasimi) whom am seeing the grace and glory of God, day in day out. To my sisters, brothers, cousins, especially to my dearest sister (Adeola Liadi) and her family in the U.K., thanks for all your contribution, encouragements and love.

Also, my acknowledges goes to my spiritual parents (Apostle Dr. Dele Johnson & Rev. Dr. Adekunbi Johnson), the founder and General overseer of Jesus Liberation Ministries worldwide, for mentoring and nurturing me in the vineyard of God to be a 'workman who accurately handles the word of truth.'

Lastly, my deepest gratitude goes to the entire JLM NY family, for the love and support towards me as their humble pastor, giving me the passion to serve Jesus Christ steadfastly, diligently and faithfully through them. I also extend my salutations to the Faculty of Gate of Heaven Theological Institute & Seminary for the tutoring, mentorship and encouragements.

Dedication

This book is dedicated to all Christians suffering persecution all over the world.

I dedicate this book to all Jesus Liberation Ministries members worldwide.

I also dedicate this book to a dear friend and brother, Mr. Akinbayo Alli, of blessed memory. We love you, but God loves you more. Continue to rest at the bosom of your maker.

Finally, I dedicate this book to all those out there pushing hard to find a path to make an impact in life.

Table of Contents

ACKNOWLEDGMENTS ... III
DEDICATION ... V
INTRODUCTION ... IX
SALVATION (THE FUNDAMENTAL OF ALL THINGS) ... 1
LIFESTYLE OR LIFE STATUS? ... 9
GRACE TO BE GROUNDED ... 15
RIGHTEOUSNESS EXALTS A NATION ... 21
GROAN, GO AND GROW ... 27
PILLARS OF SUCCESS ... 35
MAKE IMPACT AS THE SALT & LIGHT OF THE WORLD ... 43
THE PATH OF AN EAGLE ... 53
STAY ON THE RIGHT PATH TO MAKE IMPACT ... 69
FOLLOW THE PATH OF CONSISTENT FAITH ... 77
PUT YOUR GOD GIVEN GIFTS TO USE ... 85
DON'T STOP! YOU ARE MAKING A MARK ALREADY ... 93
MISTAKES YOU SHOULD NEVER MAKE ... 103
CONCLUSION ... 109
FIRST ACTION AND STEP TO TAKE ... 113
REFERENCES ... 117
SCRIPTURE INDEX ... 119

Introduction

Fading away like the stars of the morning,
Losing their light in the glorious sun.
Thus, would we pass from the earth and its toiling,
Only remembered by what we have done.

Everyone wants to leave a mark on the sands of time, but all most people ever do is be a mirage flashing across the paths of others in life. While others carve their memories upon diamonds and leave unfading indentures on the people's hearts and lives, others live and go as if they never lived.

Some lived and were never remembered, and they are quickly forgotten; others are always remembered, forever cherished. What makes the difference?

The truth is that we all make impacts. In one way or the other, we all affect the lives that come in contact with us. We touch hearts and lives and leave our marks on them by our words, gestures, actions, reactions, and even inactions. Yet, not all impacts are enviable or enduring. Some have lived and touched lives massively that their memories are gold, always surviving the furnace of the test of time, forever cherished. Some others leave memories that are better not made, such have tears, heartbreaks, evil, and all sorts of wickedness as their memorial forever.

The Bible says, *"The memory of the righteous is blessed, but the name of the wicked will rot"* – Proverbs 10:7.

We would all be remembered. The question is, what will you be remembered for? What impact and legacy will you leave? Will your memory be blessed, or will your name rot?

This and many more will be answered in this book. May this book carve golden memories in your heart and life!

May it inspire, encourage, motivate and spur you to take action to a life of impact!

Shalom,

Dr. Samuel Liadi

CHAPTER 1

Salvation
(The Fundamental of All Things)

I remember a story I heard while I was young (growing up). It was of a pig that was dressed up ever so nicely. This pig was decorated with gorgeous attire and beautiful ribbons. It was taught how to behave well, live neatly, walk like a prince, and be stately in composure. The pig was put in a beautiful house and renamed 'Prince.'

Oh! The pig tried so hard to behave well. It strove to avoid dirt and mire. It learned to be stately and regal. It did it well until everyone forgot it was a pig.

However, a day came, and the pig forgot all about its new name, the beautiful trappings of its house, and the bundles finesse it was surrounded with. The new life was too difficult for it to keep up. It escaped from the hardship and restrictions of its new life, found mire around the house, and wallowed in it until it became unrecognizable to all who knew it as Prince.

A wise man was consulted to tell everyone what could have possibly gone wrong. I find his response instructive.

"Nothing went wrong. Things only went back to normal." He said, "A pig will always be a pig no matter how finely you dress it up. You would need to recreate it if you want it to be anything but a pig." The wise man concluded.

If we ever make an impact, it will be because of the things we do, but the fact is that the things we do are just an extension of who we are. If we are only remembered by what we have done, then we should be careful about the things we do. If we would leave positive indelible marks on the lives of everyone we come across, we must do good at all times, say only the right words and have the right motives always. This would be possible if we are inherently good because we can only reason, speak, act, and react based on who we are. Unfortunately, no human can claim to be inherently good.

Jesus said in the book of Matthew 19:17 that *"…No one is good but One, that is, God…"*

This does not mean that nobody does well. A lot of people do good for whatever reason they deem fit. What Jesus meant in the above scripture is that nobody can claim to be good all-round because sometimes the good most of us do are actually born out of wrong motives, e.g., to spite someone, to get accolades or even to injure others.

Even if we succeed in being able to do good with the right motives, how many can claim to be all-round and consistently good? What we realize is that most people try to do what is good with the right motives but fail sometimes. We find that we cannot always keep up doing what is right. We were made good. We were created good, but we became corrupted when Adam, our progenitor, fell and his sinful nature was imputed in us (his descendants). Since then, humankind discovers that the willingness to do good is present, but the ability to do it is sometimes lacking.

The Apostle Paul describes this struggle accurately in **Romans 7:15-25:**

> *"For what I am doing, I do not understand. For what I will to do, that I do not practice; but what I hate, that I do. If, then, I do what I will not to do, I agree with the law that it is good. But now, it is no longer I who do it, but sin that dwells in me. For I know that in me (that is, in my flesh) nothing good dwells; for to will is present*

> with me, but how to perform what is good I do not find. For the good that I will to do, I do not do; but the evil I will not to do, that I practice. Now if I do what I will not to do, it is no longer I who do it, but sin that dwells in me. I find then a law, that evil is present with me, the one who wills to do good. For I delight in the law of God according to the inward man. But I see another law in my members, warring against the law of my mind, and bringing me into captivity to the law of sin which is in my members. O wretched man that I am! Who will deliver me from this body of death? I thank God--through Jesus Christ our Lord! So then, with the mind I myself serve the law of God, but with the flesh the law."

We need to understand that when we focus only on the things we do, we merely see the tip of the iceberg. Who we are is critical to what we do, as illustrated in the story in the opening paragraph. We can only do the good that does not emanate from within us for so long; the real nature soon comes peeking out. We could do all the good in the world, and everything would amount to nothing in the light of eternal significance if we as the doer of good are not good ourselves.

Apostle Paul captures this accurately by stating that "In me dwells no good thing." We must realize that impact begins with us, that if we would make any lasting impact, we must become good.

Matthew 12:33 *"Either make the tree good and its fruit good, or else make the tree bad and its fruit bad; for a tree is known by its fruit."*

From this passage, we see that we can become good. The significance of what Jesus said in this passage is that if we are made right in our being, our fruits, that is, the things that proceed from us (our actions, our reactions, our thoughts, our speech, our habits, our personality) will become good. We will then become good people, having a good impact on people. How do we become good?

Divine Impartation for Impact
A bad tree cannot make itself good; it needs to be made right. Goodness must be imparted into its being to make it good. An illustration from the field of agriculture readily comes to mind. Have you heard of grafting? This is how grafting is carried out.

Farmer A has two species of orange on his farm. Species A produces sweet and big oranges while species B produces poorly. Farmer A would cut the top of a tree which is of species B (this part becomes the scion) and cut the top of a tree which is of species A. He will then place the top part of species B (scion) upon the lower part of species A (rootstock) and bind it up. This new tree carrying sweet and big species A as its root and poorly producing species B on the top would then begin producing sweet and big oranges just like species A.

This is what happens at salvation. God engrafts us into Christ, and we become good like Him. He imputed and imparts us with the righteousness and goodness of Christ that we may become carriers of Christlikeness. We then begin to do what is good like Him and impact our world as He did. An unsaved person has nothing good of real value to offer the world. If we would make a good and lasting impact, we must seek, find, and accept the gift of salvation.

Receiving the Gift of Salvation

Salvation is by grace through faith. Receiving the gift of salvation is not herculean. All you need to do is allow grace and then, believe. Grace is the means through which God works changes in the heart of men. Faith is what sets the work in motion.

The Bible emphatically stated in **Ephesians 2:8** that *"For by grace you have been saved through faith, and that not of yourselves; it is the gift of God."*
To have faith is to:
- Believe that you need salvation
- Believe that you can only find it salvation in Christ Jesus

- Believe that God is faithful to His promise to save you as you call upon Him.

The means through which the work of salvation is carried out in man is Grace.

Titus 2:11 *"For the grace of God that brings salvation has appeared to all men, teaching us that, denying ungodliness and wordly lusts, we should live soberly, righteously, and godly in the present age."*

The role of grace in salvation is like that of a teacher. Once you believe, grace begins to teach you how to live, act, reason, and react. As you allow grace to guide you and as you yield to his teachings, you will find the ability to do good and right, and your new grace lifestyle will leave a lasting and positive impact on the lives around you.

Apostle Paul exemplifies this in his statement in **1 Cor. 15:10** which states, *"But by the grace of God I am what I am, and His grace toward me was not in vain; but I labored more abundantly than they all, yet not I, but the grace of God which was with me."* From this passage, we see the tripartite relationship of life-status, lifestyle, and grace. Most Christians look at Apostle Paul and envy him. They envy his calling, his achievements for God, his eternal impact, etc. All they see is the status he has attained. They do not take note of his lifestyle neither do they consider his submission to grace. Let me further explain the three (3) relationship of life-status, lifestyle, and grace as regards to Apostle Paul in the above Bible verse:

1. **"...I am who I am..."** – this is referring to his status. All that he was that we admire and wish to get without considering the other two parts that make him what we envy.

2. **"...I labored abundantly..."** – this is the lifestyle that birthed the status. We want to have an impact like Paul, but we don't want to labor. That will never work!

3. **"Grace"** – Twice, he referred to the grace of God as the bedrock of it all. Grace was working in him, and he was living it out.

Stop chasing after status and begin to pay attention to your lifestyle while staying under the tutelage of the grace of God. Your status will automatically begin to improve!

CHAPTER 2

Lifestyle or Life Status?

I once heard the story of a wealthy man who embarked on a journey with his slave. Before setting out, the slave made a request. He told his master that he didn't want to be treated like a slave. He wanted his master to introduce him to people as his son. His master agreed, they set out, and he was dressed up in a beautiful finery. They then got to a place where there was a feast, and as previously agreed, his master introduced him as his son until he misbehaved!

While the feast and festivity were going on, someone spotted him in the kitchen, eating from the trash can! His master was told, "Sir, your son, was found eating from the trash can outdoors…" "No, he is not my son. He is just a slave." The man quickly responded. The slave asked, "Why did you break our agreement? Why did you let them know the truth? His master replied, "you caused it. You stopped acting like a son and acted like a slave."

Many of us are like the slave in this story. We are so concerned about our status in life, but we pay little or no attention to our lifestyle. The truth is people will always treat us and view us in the light of whatever impression they have of us. Your lifestyle predominantly determines your status in life. It makes sense, therefore, that you should pay attention to your lifestyle, i.e., how you live.

Have you heard the saying, "The first impression matters most?" This famous saying is a gem that everyone who would make an impact must always keep in mind. When people say that the first impression matters most, they mean to say that the first set of behaviors people read, may affect their perspective about you forever. This may either be your speech, your comportment, your body language, your dressing, your attitude and reactions to issues, etc.

The scary thing about first impressions is that they are usually unconsciously made. In most cases, people have their first impressions about us while we are totally unaware that they are watching us while they are already forming their opinions about us. This impression will be the basis for their opinion about us and the status we get assigned to in their minds. That is the more reason we, as believers, must live upright and continue to strive for righteous and holy living both in private and in public, because you never know who is watching you as a yardstick to follow Christ. Always remember that your action and reaction are the first tools of evangelism, they can attract people to Christ, and also dispel people from Christ.

"Then the shepherds came and drove them away; but Moses stood up and helped them, and watered their flock. When they came to Reuel their father, he said, "How is it that you have come so soon today?" And they said, "An Egyptian delivered us from the hand of the shepherds, and he also drew enough water for us and watered the flock." **– Exodus 2:17-19**

In these Bible passages, we did not see Moses introducing himself to the daughters of Jethro, but they told their father that he was an Egyptian. How did they come to that conclusion? They must have noted his speech, his dressing, probably his carriage, his mannerisms, etc. Noting all these things and maybe many more about him, they concluded that he was an Egyptian and told their father so. Why the certainty in describing him as an Egyptian? This is so because of the first impression they had of him, even though Moses, was an Israelite, was called an Egyptian.

You might be a nice and benevolent person and expect people to treat you as such, but if the impression people have of you is otherwise, no one will treat you as such. You must live according to the status you desire. As a Christian, you must live as a Christian (model Christlikeness). On the other hand, if you want to be wealthy and successful, you must find out what the habit, principles, dedication and perseverance of wealthy and successful people are and begin to live and follow those principles. You cannot attain any status beyond your lifestyle.

Your lifestyle would either make or mar you. It may open doors for you or shut them. So, be careful how you live! Don't just live anyhow and expect to be great in life. It will never happen! Even those who dive into crime to amass wealth, mostly ends up at the bottom stacks of life with no meaningful impact on themselves or the world around them.

Study the lives of great men and pattern your life after theirs. Do a case study of great men in the bible and genuine men of God and model your life after them.

How you live is who you are. Greatness does not come by chance; it is premeditated. You must begin to live deliberately. To live deliberately is to live purposefully. That means that you don't live or act impulsively. Everything you do always must be geared towards the achievement of that status you have in mind. And by aligning your will to God's purpose for your life, you will certainly make a great impact in life.

(Jesus is the ultimate role model. Always remember that you are the 'first bible people read' – Author)

CHAPTER 3

Grace to Be Grounded

An important man was invited to a function, on arriving at the venue. He looked round to scan the faces of people present at the ceremony to see if there was anyone as important, dignified as himself. Finding none, he proceeded to seat himself on the most prestigious seat present. Who could it have been prepared for, if not him?

Imagine his utter dismay then, when he was later ushered from the highest seat to the least seat when more important dignitaries arrived. He finally found himself at the least seat. He had tried to take the best position, but instead, he was relegated to the worst. He tried to make himself fly but ended up becoming grounded.

You need the grace to fly, to soar as high as possible. If you try to make yourself fly, you will be grounded, unable to even leave the spot.

Grace is the divine ability imparted into a man to do what he otherwise could not do. You need grace if you would fly and soar. Only those who realize that they cannot go far without grace will find mercy. Those who humble themselves enough to receive grace would rise!

Well-Grounded to Avoid Becoming Grounded

This subheading is much more than just a play of words. The fact is that if the grace of God does not ground you well, you will become grounded, unable to fly or soar.

Grace will keep you grounded so that you may not be grounded. This is another way of saying grace makes you so wise and sensible, so balanced in life and living, that you cannot but soar!

1 Peter 5:10 *"But may the God of all grace, who called us to His eternal glory by Christ Jesus, after you have suffered a while, perfect, establish, strengthen, and settle you."* From this bible passage, grace will do the following things:

1. **Perfect you:** This means that grace will work on your inadequacies and shortcomings. It will deal

with every character flaw that will impede your soaring. Every weight that will drag you down will be cut off. This is the part of the process grace takes you through to ensure you are well-grounded.
2. **Establish you:** Grace will give you a genuine foundation to build a solid life that will not crash at the slightest hint of trouble or challenges. It will set your feet on the path that leads to excellence. The path may seem rough to many, but it will lead to glory for your life.

3. **Strengthen you:** Grace will give you all the stamina you need to succeed and soar! It will use various situations and circumstances, which may be hard or easy to build into you, a strength of character that is uncommon.

4. **Settle you:** Grace leads you into bliss and let you grow roots so that your place in the circle of the great is forever sealed. It gives you a permanent seat in the circle of the successful.

This kind of grounding grace gives what makes you rise, fly, and never to be grounded. It is the process grace takes those who submit to it through a new life in Christ. When this is achieved, you will never be grounded by anything. Nothing will be able to hold you down from soaring high into your glorious destiny.

Philippians 4:11-13 says, *"Not that I speak in regard to need, for I have learned in whatever state I am, to be content: I know how to be abased, and I know how to abound. Everywhere and in all things I have learned both to be full and to be hungry, both to abound and to suffer need. I can do all things through Christ who strengthens me".*

A lot of people skip the preceding verses of this passage and jump to **Philippians 4: 13**. Every day they confess that they can do all things, but when you look at them, all you see is incapacities. They are unable to soar. Negative situations get them down easily, while circumstances turn them into horrible people. They cannot ride the waves as the eagle. They are always under, never above. When they face little difficulties, they become grounded, unable to move, unable to function. What is missing? They have missed the grounding process of grace. They are not well-grounded; they lack the strength of character.

The bible passage above is the confession of one who is well-grounded by grace and in grace has soared and is soaring. He has humbly submitted to the tutelage of grace. He has learned to master situations and circumstances rather than being mastered by them. He had learned to ride his storms and soar like an eagle. Those who do not submit to be grounded by grace will find themselves grounded, unable to fly or soar.

Those who couldn't wait for the process, who would rather jump into quick results and shortcuts, rather than wait duly for the process, will find themselves grounded. The passage above earnestly warned that those who try to make themselves fly or soar would be grounded. Learn to wait for your time and season. Don't try to cut corners or make yourself what you are not. There is no shortcut to excellent results; the due process must take place. Allow grace to develop and make you well-grounded, lest you become grounded.

CHAPTER 4

Righteousness Exalts A Nation

I once read a Chinese folklore about a king who was searching for a successor because he had no children. One day, all the young boys in the kingdom were brought into the palace to examine them and to find one who would be a suitable successor for the king. Each one had prepared hard to answer difficult questions, be of best behavior, etc. Some dressed in a manner befitting a prince; others came simply. Expectations were high, but the old king simply gave each of them a seed to plant and nurture. They were to bring the resulting plant to the palace after some weeks. How would they handle the affairs of the kingdom if they couldn't nurture a little seed to flourish? They all went away determined to pass this test.

Righteousness exalts a nation

A little boy from a poor home was there. He determined to nurture the seed to life. He watered the seed appropriately, ensured the right amount of sunshine, and provided all conditions necessary for germination. He carefully did everything he could think of, but his seed refused to germinate. Whenever he went out with his mother, his mates would tell him how well theirs were doing. It seemed he was the only one failing the test.

Exhibition day came, and every other boy had beautiful plants to show. Some were flowering; some were so tall. The boy wept as he discovered that he alone had failed the test. Other boys laughed out loud at him when they saw his empty jar. They all tagged their pots and put them in a designated place for inspection. They all kept laughing at the boy until the king announced him as the winner!

It turned out that all the others had cheated! They were all given dead seeds! Only the boy was honest enough to admit his "failure." The others had all found another seed to plant when they noticed theirs were not growing. Some had bought the beautiful tender plants they presented as theirs. The boy was named successor, and he grew up to be a wise and famous king who was well-loved by all and sundry.

It was Solomon the wisest king of Israel who said in his biblical book of Proverbs that *"righteousness exalts a nation and sin is a reproach to anyone"* – Proverbs 14:34.

It is usually said that 'honesty is the best policy.' It is a pity, however, to see how morally low many would stoop to appear to be what they are not. Righteousness is not a popular policy in the world we live in today, but it is still the best.

Many people would gladly sacrifice integrity on the altar to become affluent. What they do not know is that such affluence does not last. The Bible stated categorically in **Proverbs 20:17** that *"Bread gained by deceit is sweet to a man, but afterward his mouth will be filled with gravel."*

When you are enjoying something you gained deceitfully, you feel happy and smart. You inwardly pat yourself on the back, who else is as intelligent? What you don't know is that action and reaction are two forces opposite in direction but equal in magnitude. That is Newton's law of motion, by the way. Someone jokingly added this "But a reaction is usually greater in magnitude than action."

What that simply means is, 'Payback is usually harsher and more difficult.' For example, assuming you slap someone, and another person was asked to make you feel the pain of the slap exactly how it felt to the one you hit. Who decides the magnitude of pain to be inflicted on you as payback? One may insist that cutting off your arm is the only reparation for the pain inflicted.

Cain killed Abel and felt he had covered it up until God came demanding for his brother. The penalty of his sin was so high that he said: "The punishment for my sin is greater than I can bear." – **Genesis 4:13**. I'm sure Cain didn't think there would be consequences when he did what he did.

The Bible says it this way: *"We know that God causes everything to work together for the good of those who love God and are called according to his purpose for them"* – **Romans 8:28**.

This bible passage doesn't necessarily mean that everything in your life will be good. But rather what it means is that when you put your whole life together, every piece of it works together for good. It's like making a cake. You may not like the taste of each ingredient that makes up the cake itself, but when it's all put together, it comes out tasting good. This also doesn't mean everything works together like we want it to or that every story will have a happy ending. The fact of life is that not every business decision will make a million dollars. Not every couple that gets married lives happily ever after. Not every child will become captain of the football team. Instead, this bible verse is a reminder to us that we can have absolute confidence that God causes everything to work together for the good *of those who love Him.* Since God's plan is always good, according to Jeremiah 29:11, we believers can be rest assured with the confidence that, no matter our circumstances or situations, God is active and will conclude things according to His good, wise plans and design. So, the best thing to do always is to surrender and align our will to His perfect will and continue to live righteously. **1 John 5:14-15** *"This is the confidence we have in approaching God: that if we ask anything according to his will, he hears us. And if we know that he hears us—whatever we ask—we know that we have what we asked of him."*

Your decision to align your will with God's and to always trust Him will be rewarded. The Bible says, *"...God is able to do exceedingly abundantly above all that we ask or think, according to the power that worketh in us"* – **Ephesians 3:20**

The master key here is if you desire to make an impact in life, follow righteousness. Let righteousness be the guiding principle in all you do. **1 John 2:29** says, *"if you know that He is righteous, you know that everyone who practices righteousness is born of Him."*

Let these principles guide you always:

1. Give God priority always. Keep Him at the center continuously.
2. Do right always, even if it will cost you dearly.
3. Speak the truth always, even if they will cut your tongue.
4. Do to others as you would want them to do to you.
5. Admit your errors and failures always; it does not reduce you.
6. Never cover up your mistakes or sin. Confess them, be honest with God, yourself, and others.

It is stated in **Psalm 106:3** that "Blessed are those who keep justice, And he who does righteousness at all times!"

CHAPTER 5

Groan, Go and Grow

When Mrs. A. discovered she was pregnant, she was filled with exultant joy; a new life was being formed right inside her! To her, it was magical until morning sickness hit. Waves of nausea would prevent her from eating. When her pregnancy advanced, she couldn't shake the feeling that she looked like an hippopotamus. She avoided the mirror altogether. The heartburn she felt grew worse by the day. One word qualified how she felt all day long - discomfort! Then, the delivery day arrived. Ah! The pain was out of this world. Surviving the pain took her breath away. Sometimes, she would squeeze the bedposts as if her life depended on it, while trying to push as the midwives directed. She groaned and grunted! She pushed and pushed and pushed. Out came the baby! Although her body felt as if she had been run over twice by a moving truck, she smiled triumphantly. She looked at her baby, and all the discomfort and pain faded into obscurity. She had birthed a new life. And that was all that mattered!

When you get the results you've been waiting for, the pain of the process will fade away. We all know this, but that does not in any way reduce the intensity of the pain while the process is still ongoing. What do you do before the results come? You persevere and bear the pain. Similarly, to grow, you must groan and go! There is no shortcut to success.

Tai Solarin, the late African intellectual giant, titled his now-famous speech of January 1st, 1964, **"May Your Road Be Rough."** In his speech, he wished that there be plenty of troubles for his listeners that year, because as he noted, "Our successes are conditioned by the amount of risks we are ready to take."

Difficulties have a way of making humans better; when you are going through hardship, your faculties are engaged, and you find that solutions abound around you. Business empires have been built, great books have been written, and beautiful songs have been composed when adversities forced people to find a solution.

Groaning Is Allowed (Groan That You May Grow)
It's okay to groan when you find yourself in an adverse situation. Take a very good look at the situation and see

how wrong and how bad things are and be provoked. Let your inner man be provoked. Shed tears if you want; it has its place. You see, when your adversities don't provoke you within, when you don't feel the pain of the bad situation you are in, you can't grow out of it. There is fire on the mountain when your adversities do not provoke your spirit. It means you have accepted it as your lot. It means you have given in to your circumstance, and once you've given in, you cannot get out. You cannot get out of your adverse situation if it does not provoke you. Please, get provoked! Groan, until your inner man gets provoked! This is my first interpretation of the word "groan."

Once you are provoked, don't stay silent! Cry out to God! Groan in prayer to Him who can do exceedingly, abundantly above all you can ever ask or think! Let God hear your groaning!

Jeremiah 33:1-3 says *"Moreover, the word of the Lord came to Jeremiah a second time, while he was still shut up in the court of the prison, saying, "Thus says the Lord who made it, the Lord who formed it to establish it (the Lord is His name): 'Call to Me, and I will answer you, and show you great and mighty things, which you do not know."*

Look at the divine instruction to Jeremiah. God asked him to call out to Him. The promise of receiving the revelation of high and mighty things is premised on 'calling on God.' There is a saying that "when you are shut up in prison, don't shut up your mouth." This is well put in **Psalm 81:10** "*I am the Lord your God, Who brought you up out of the land of Egypt. Open your mouth wide and I will fill it*". This is a divine command to open your mouth wide so God can fill it. Don't close your mouth. Keep believing, keep praying. Pray without ceasing! Pray until something happens. Groan to God that you may grow. This is my second interpretation of groaning.

Don't Just Groan, Go!
Many people like Mrs. A. in the introductory story rejoice when they conceive a new idea, when they begin a new project or when they start at a new job. They enthusiastically talk about it and happily plan for it until the going gets tough. Execution becomes a problem. Then, they begin to drag their feet, murmur, and feel like quitting. The truth is that nothing good comes easy. If it pays, you must pay for it! You have taken a good look at your situation and have decided you want a change. That's good, but don't sit still, waiting for change to happen. Make it happen. This is going!

Move! Don't sit bemoaning and glorifying your lot! Take action. Do something. Execute your plan. Go out. Meet people. Ask questions. It's alright if you cannot fly, run. Even if you cannot run, walk. Let's assume you cannot walk, crawl. If that is impossible, find something or somebody to drag or carry you. By all means, move! Don't stay in the same place. Think of Jack Ma, the business guru that birthed Alibaba, AliExpress, and some other giant online stores. He was forced into creating that when he noticed how difficult it was for him to get Chinese products online. He simply went and created an avenue to solve the problem he encountered. That hardship you are complaining of might just be an opportunity to shine in disguise. Success is simply the ability to find a solution to a problem. If there is no problem to be solved, there can be no invention.

For some time now, I have been facing some challenges in my personal life, and I was meditating (frankly, inwardly complaining) on how limited resources I seem to have to achieve what I need to make. I was grumbling inwardly. As I continued grumbling, the parable of our Lord Jesus Christ about the unprofitable servant flashed into my mind, and I realized something I had never realized. The master gave talents to his servants. One received five; another received two; the last was given just one. At first glance, it seemed the master was partial. But, notice the basis for the distribution, "according to their ability." The master knew the ability of each of them. He knew this particular servant had such greatness in him that could produce results even with one talent! The master knew that one talent was enough for him to shine! The painful thing is the servant couldn't see the opportunity in his pain! He didn't see the privilege his predicament was bestowing on him. All he could think of was how little the resources he was given is.

As I meditated on this passage, the Lord asked me, "do you know this servant could have gained up to fifty more talents with his one talent?" He could have outshined the ones who received more than him if he had applied himself to do so! I wonder the kind of accolades he would have gotten if he used his one talent and gained five or ten! Even if he gained three, his percentage increase is higher than the one who had five and gained five more. Just imagine the glory of using limited resources to accomplish much.

If you take a good look around you, you will find that some people you envy, their results have fewer resources than you in creating those results! If you would apply your heart to wisdom, you will find that you can achieve more significant results than some who seem to have more resources than you. Stop concentrating on your pain! Groan all you want but remember to go! Act. Take action!

This is how Apostle Paul summarized it all in **Philippians 4:6-7** "Be anxious for nothing, but in everything by prayer and supplication, with thanksgiving, let your requests be made known to God; [7] and the peace of God, which surpasses all understanding, will guard your hearts and minds through Christ Jesus"

CHAPTER 6

Pillars of Success

A church building project was in progress in a rural area that was a bit unfriendly to the gospel. The land was purchased, and a small building was erected with wooden built pillars. The brethren (Christians) continued holding their services oblivious of the fact that the land they constructed their Church on was termite infested. One day the church leader felt nudged by the Spirit to change the pillars to metal. The action was expedited quickly. In the process of changing the pillars, they discovered that termites had eaten up the base of the pillar! The building would have come down crashing on their heads. They later got to know that some of the unbelieving natives knew about the termite infestation and were eagerly expecting when the building would collapse. There were rumors in some parts of the town that the building had collapsed! The timely inspection of their pillars and the quick corrective action taken is what saved them from the disaster.

Psalm 11:3 affirmed that "If the foundations be destroyed, what can the righteous do?"

In everything we do, whether physically or spiritually, there must be a foundation and pillar of support. It is the foundation and pillars of a building that will determine if a building will be stable and durable. As a matter of fact, if there is a structural defect or problem in a building, the engine doesn't look elsewhere but at the foundation and pillars of the building. This is the same with man. If the foundation of a man is faulty, where you look for a solution determines if the purpose of God will be fulfilled in the life of the person or not.

No building is stronger than its pillars. Weak pillars spell doom! When building success in life, you must ensure your pillars and foundation are topnotch, of the best materials that can withstand heat, flood, storm, pressure, adversity, and whatever comes against it, because tests will surely come and if the pillars are not strong enough, the building will certainly crumble. What you must do is prepare ahead for them by putting the right things in place. Anybody can build an edifice; what matters is building a lasting edifice that will stand the test of time. A structure that will never fade out of relevance is what you must strive to build.

Once a person is born, he starts to build, consciously or unconsciously. All his choices, decisions, indecisions, attitude, habits, actions, and reactions are the building materials with which he is building his life. The fact is that everyone is building; some may be aware or not. But it's best that you build consciously and be aware that every action and reaction, every thought, every decision, every habit you choose to allow or disallow are what will culminate into the structure of your life. If you decide to build consciously, you will allow only the best materials in constructing your life. This implies that you will examine every decision, every choice, every action, every attitude, etc., to ensure that only the best is what you are allowing in your life.

Apostle Paul: The Master-builder

If anyone ever deserves the title of "Master-builder," Apostle Paul is such a man. If there is anyone who built a lasting structure that has a colossal impact in Christendom, again, Apostle Paul is the man. His works, his words still stand till today, and they will continue to stand for evermore. If we would follow the footsteps of anyone in building right, Paul is the master-builder to look up to as a role model. He gave his all for the course of following Christ and his impact will be forever felt.

1 Corinthians 3:10-15

According to the grace of God which was given to me, as a wise master builder I have laid the foundation, and another builds on it. But let each one take heed how he builds on it. For no other foundation can anyone lay than that which is laid, which is Jesus Christ. Now if anyone builds on this foundation with gold, silver, precious stones, wood, hay, straw, each one's work will become clear; for the Day will declare it, because it will be revealed by fire; and the fire will test each one's work, of what sort it is. If anyone's work which he has built on it endures, he will receive a reward. If anyone's work is burned, he will suffer loss; but he himself will be saved, yet so as through fire.

In this passage, we see Paul giving a hint of his building material. His foundation was Jesus Christ. That guaranteed the success of his building project. Paul went ahead to tell us the different materials with which people build these days.

Some use the best materials at a high cost to themselves. These are meticulous people who approve only of excellence in their lives. To these people, 'Is it right?' Is it not enough? "Is it good?' They go on to ask, 'Is this the best?' They permit only excellent thoughts, accurate actions, unique reactions, etc. These are the builders with gold. Some build with silver and precious stones. They do what is right at great cost to themselves. They do not indulge themselves. They go to extra lengths to do what is right. They are uncommon and unique people. They stand out. They shine for God wherever they find themselves.

However, there are others who build with wood, hay, and stubble. These are the people who go easy on themselves. They would do nothing that would cost them much. They shy away from hardship and adversity. They allow anything and indulge themselves in insensibility. They are ordinary people. They do nothing, sacrifice nothing, and achieve nothing. Don't be like this set of people.

Check yourself now. What material are you building with? How much are you prepared to sacrifice to become what you should become? Are you not living in self-indulgence, sitting doing nothing, expecting situations to take care of themselves? Are you living life consciously or unconsciously? Be wise; emulate Paul, the master-builder! Join the league of builders with gold, silver, and precious stones.

The bible passage above also tells us what to expect after building. The test of time must inspect your work. Consider this, how many of these building materials can stand the test of fire? Real gold fears no fire, fire purifies gold and silver, and improves its brilliance, but what of wood, hay, and stubble? They will only feed the fire, and after the fire, nothing but ashes will be left of them. Choose your building materials wisely.

Jesus: The Chief Cornerstone

One major reason people's destiny doesn't manifest is because they have built their faith on the wrong pillar of support. And even when they realized their foundation is faulty, they look everywhere but not unto Jesus. Sometimes we build our foundation on the pillar of human support; on people, worldly powers, education, money/wealth, etc. All this will fail and cannot withstand the test of time. There is only one sure foundation and pillar of support you can build on. Apostle Paul points this out in **1 Corinthians 3:11**: that, *"For no other foundation can anyone lay than that which is laid, which is Jesus Christ."*

Jesus is the pillar and the solid foundation that we can build on that will never ever fail, shake nor crumble. And the goodness is that once you have given your life to Christ, no matter how faulty your foundation may be, He will fix, deal and deliver you, and your life will be on the path of success.

Ephesians 2:20 *"Having been built on the foundation of the apostles and prophets, Jesus Christ Himself being the chief cornerstone."*

If you will build your life, choose Christlikeness as your pillars. Emulate the life of Jesus, and you will find that your life, like His, would be a lasting edifice.

1. **Emulate His Integrity:**
   - The integrity of Jesus! His accusers could not substantiate their accusations. Nothing he did could be pointed out as wrong. They tried hard but couldn't malign Him. Two godless kings cross-examined him and declared Him innocent of all charges and accusations levied against Him.
   - Let integrity be the pillar of your life. People may dislike you, but don't let them be able to pinpoint any evil to you. Let there be no corruption, no dishonesty, no crime found in you.

2. **Emulate His Consistency:**
The writer of the book of Acts said something about Jesus, which cannot be said of many of us. Jesus began to do and teach the same thing until His ascension. He didn't stop doing what He came to do. He persevered in the face of opposition and kept at what He was sent to do. Many of us start to do something, but we stop along the way. Make it your principle today to always finish whatever you begin. Don't stop projects halfway. Always go through. Be consistent and persevere to the end. Let consistency and perseverance be the pillars of your life. This is the only way to true success.

3. Emulate His Holiness:
Jesus lived a pious, holy and God-pleasing life. He did only those things that please God. Even Satan could point at nothing ungodly in Jesus (as God in the flesh) – this is godliness at its peak! Let devotion be the pillar of your life. This is what real success entails.

4. Emulate His Simplicity:
He is God; He lived as a servant. He lived in such a humble and simple manner that poor people could approach Him, and such humility and moderation also make the rich approachable to Him. He was balanced in simplicity and moderation. Therefore, choose simplicity, humble yourself and dispel pride.

5. Emulate His Finishing:
Jesus achieved the purpose of His coming to the world. He completed His assignment. He didn't abscond from his duties and responsibilities. Determine to finish well.

These are the pillars of success, as seen in Jesus-the most successful man that ever lived. If you examine the lives of other outstanding people, you will find these principles at work in them all. Choose integrity always, be consistent and pious. Decide for simplicity and ensure you finish well. You can't miss success if you do.

CHAPTER 7

Make Impact as The Salt & Light of The World

Matthew 5:13-16 *"You are the salt of the earth, but if salt has lost its taste, how shall its saltiness be restored? It is no longer good for anything except to be thrown out and trampled under people's feet. "You are the light of the world. A city set on a hill cannot be hidden. Nor do people light a lamp and put it under a basket, but on a stand, and it gives light to all in the house. In the same way, let your light shine before others so that they may see your good works and give glory to your Father who is in heaven".*

The path to successfully make a memorable and eternal impact is to be a signpost to eternity by pointing people to God, by being salt and light to the world. Once you already got Jesus as your Lord and Savior, He empowers you to lead others to follow Him. Also, your readiness and commitment to His service, obeying His commandments in all spheres, and not holding back your God-given gifts and talents to satisfy the needs of humanity, is what sets you on the path of making a long-lasting impact that will stand the test of time.

Let me paraphrase the opening bible passage (Matthew 5:13-16) with the view to explaining our position as the salt and light of this world in the following way:

You're here to be salt (seasoning) that brings out the God-flavors in this world. If you lose your saltiness, how will the world (people) taste godliness? You've lost your usefulness, purpose and will end up in the garbage. Also, you're here to be the light, shining forth the glory of God in this world.

Jesus used the metaphorical term 'salt and light' to liken us mainly because of the distinctive qualities in salt and light; they have immense influence; instant impact; easily noticed; hard to conceal, and they are both ubiquitous in nature.

The term "You are the salt of the earth..." – Matthew 5:13 is commonly quoted to attribute special characteristics worthy of exemplification. This narrative can be traced back to the ancient time when salt was commonly used as a means of paying salary to people in the Roman empire, as a matter of fact, the English word "salary" was coined out from the Latin word '*salarium*,' which literally means 'salt-money.' This is often carried into conversation, when they say, "that man is not worth his salt," that means 'the man is worthlessness,' which substantiates the high value and significance ascribed to salt in bible eras.

Jesus also referred to us as the light of the world in the same perspective. Truly our light as Christians reflect the light of Christ that disperses darkness. It's like being in a dark room, and all of a sudden the electric light was turned on, the transformation reveals everything in the room and gives you the awareness of where you are and everything around you. In the same manner, Jesus's presence in our lives reveals the true light that illuminates our darkness. The transformation and regeneration of the light of Christ in us is so powerful that darkness can't comprehend or overcome it. The bible confirms this in **John 1:5** that *"and the light shines in the darkness and the darkness did not comprehended it."*

Let me further draw an analogy from the story I read from Rick Ezell's Sermon series:

> *"A quiet forest dweller lived high above an Austrian village along the eastern slopes of the Alps. The old gentleman had been hired many years ago by a young town council to clear away the debris from the pools of water up in the mountain crevices that fed the lovely spring flowing through their town. With faithful, silent regularity, he patrolled the hills, removed the leaves and branches, and wiped away the silt that would otherwise obstruct and*

contaminate the fresh flow of water. By and by, the village became a popular attraction for vacationers. Swans floated along the crystal-clear spring, mill wheels of various businesses located along the water, farmlands were naturally irrigated, and the view from restaurants was attractive beyond description.

Years passed. One evening the town council met for its semi-annual meeting. As they reviewed the budget, one man's eye caught the salary figure being paid the obscure keeper of the spring. Said the keeper of the purse, "Who is the old man? Why do we keep him on year after year? No one ever sees him. For all we know the strange ranger of the hills is doing us no good. He isn't necessary any longer!" By a unanimous vote, they terminate the old man's services.

For several weeks nothing changed. By early autumn, the trees began to shed their leaves. Small branches broke off and fell into the pools, hindering the rushing flow of sparkling water. One afternoon someone noticed a slight yellowish-brown color in the spring. A couple of days later, the water was much darker. Within another week, a greasy layer covered sections of the water along the banks, and a foul odor was soon detected. The mill wheels moved slower, and some finally ground to a halt. Swans left, as did the tourists. Clammy fingers of disease and sickness reached deeply into the village. Quickly, the embarrassed council called an emergency meeting.

> *Realizing their gross error in judgment, they hired back the old keeper of the spring. Within a few weeks, the veritable river of life began to clear up. The wheels started to turn, and new life returned to the hamlet in the Alps once again."*

We can take a cue from this story because it conveys significant similarities in relation to the world we live as Christians. Analogously what the old man (keeper of the springs) meant to the village is what we Christians mean to the entire world. We may appear to be inconsequential, dispensable, and minute to the cosmic world, but the fact is that no society can exist without the influence of Christians. Because we are the salt of the world, our saltiness seasoned the world and our light illuminates in an effective way that the world cannot do without. In other words, our call as followers of Jesus Christ is to become a difference maker, pathfinder, model of Christ and leaders, because we are Jesus's representative, entrusted with the sole responsibility to influence and impact the world, just like the old man in the story above.

It is our uniqueness that makes a difference in the world. The perfect righteousness and holiness imputed in us by Christ is what sets us apart and stands us out from the rest of the people, that is the distinguishing factor about us as Christians. Blaise Pascal – the French mathematician, physicist, inventor, writer and theologian, said, *"The serene, silent beauty of a holy life is the most powerful influence in the world, next to the might of God."*

However, if you are not impacting the world, then the world is impacting you. If you are not salting the world, the world is polluting you. And to prevent the world system from negatively affecting you, you must be true to your commitment and live a Christocentric lifestyle. It is then you can make a great impact that will stand the test of time. And the most legacy or impact you can make in any life is to lead them to Christ, as Jesus commissioned in **Matthew 28:19** that *"Go and make disciples of all the nations . . ."* Which is the greatest commission ever given to believers to impact the world. Consequently, Jesus expects the whole world to perceive the sensation of your salty seasoning influences and feel the lighting impact you make as the journey of your salvation progresses.

At one point or the other in our lives, we discover that we want to help change the world. That feeling is quite natural because we are all wired to be altruistic in nature. Although an effectual change is not something instantaneous, but real impact can take time. So, therefore, to make an impact and make the world a better place often starts with you changing just one person's world, and the multiplier effect of that singular act has the potential to improve other lives for generations. Some people believe that to make an impact in life involves you making a far-reaching transformation in the political and government arena. This isn't completely true because many individuals have changed the world not by concentrating on changing whole nations or entire populace, but most of the time, they concentrate on changing what is within their domain.

For example, let's look at the incident of Rosa Louise McCauley Parks – the American activist in the civil rights movement. Rosa Parks refused to surrender her seat to a white passenger on a segregated bus in Montgomery, Alabama. The point in this story is that her action wasn't aiming to change the entire world. She just took small action against what she considered unjust, immoral and unethical and yet that singular act impacted and helped change the world. Her boldness sparked the Montgomery Bus Boycott; its success launched nationwide efforts that ended racial segregation of public facilities.

The moral of this story is that making an impact and changing the world don't necessarily need enormous acts or actions. Sometimes all it takes is to focus within your locality, doing so might bring about the change you desire on a broader level, just like Rosa Parker. You don't always have to focus on changing the world from a global perspective, rather start small. Because all your good acts will certainly add-up and culminate into a lifelong change that will impact generations yet unborn.

Additionally, you can make a better and greater impact by putting more effort to impact what is around you than focusing on vast governmental and public structures already in existence. Know quite well that you can impact the world, starting right now, and it all begins with you by changing you!

Mohandas Karamchand Gandhi, the popular Indian lawyer, anti-colonial nationalist, said, *"Be the change you wish to see in the world."* This inspirational statement from Mahatma Gandhi is a reminder to us that we all have the power and ability to make impact, because whatever we do now can become a meaningful and lifelong impact; locally or globally, physically or spiritually.

Albert Einstein – the German-born theoretical physicist, said, *"Try not to become a person of success, but rather try to become a person of value."* This is so true because our value is linked to our success, the more valued you become, the more success you'll achieve. In the same manner, value is related to impact. When value grows, your impact also grows. And vehemently, you will become valuable, successful and your impacts become felt greatly. More so, great men who make the most impact are those that found or discovered their purpose and followed it faithfully with determination to succeed. When you're driven by purpose, it substantially adds value to you and other people's lives. It's quite impossible to add any notable value to anyone or impact them if you yourself have not discovered your purpose in life. Because it is purpose that kindles the desire which sustains your motivation, inspiration and makes you focused.

If you have big dreams and purpose, surely, you'll make a great impact. But first and foremost, you must know the will and purpose of God for your life, then faithfully align your will, **your ambition, aspirations, intentions,** toward God, by focusing on God's purposefulness for your life. Always pray without ceasing, asking God for strength and wisdom to persist in the face of any challenges and distraction by carnal and worldly activities. Also, never forget that your goal is to make a world felt impact both physically and spiritually.

Lastly, you must build your circle of influence (physically or spiritually) on the basis of reference to God. Always aim to strengthen your relationship with God continually. Then you'll be able to see people with the view to better understand their potentials and setbacks from the right perspective. This will make you have an accurate knowledge of your role and purpose as an influencer and impact maker.

Let Jesus be your motivating factor to preserve you every day. Envision Jesus telling you when you get to heaven: *"Well done, good and faithful servant"* – Matthew 25:21.

Now go out there and make a positive impact! Don't settle for less! It is your destiny to be a difference-maker. Be the salt that gives the world taste and be the light of Christ that illuminates the world.

CHAPTER 8

The Path of An Eagle

I once read a story about a farmer, who while returning home from his farm on a large mountainside, saw an eagle's nest. He took an egg from the nest and put the egg among his chicken eggs. After a while, the eggs were hatched. That began the life of the eagle as a chicken. He was raised as a chicken, pecking around in the dirt for grains and insects. The eagle loved his home and family, but something within it cried out for more. One day, the eagle noticed a group of eagles soaring high in the skies.

Oh! I wish I could fly like those birds, he cried. But his chicken family busted into laughter, "You can never fly like them. Those are eagles, but you are a chicken. Chickens do not fly." The eagle continued staring at his real family and wishing he could be like them. Each time he talked about his dream to fly; he was told it couldn't be done. So, he stopped dreaming about it. After a while, a mighty storm arose while the eagle was out pecking grains with his chicken family. They all shrieked in fright and took to flight. The eagle noticed, he flew higher than the rest, the more he tried the higher and higher he went. After a while, he noticed, instead of being dragged down by the storm, his flight was being boosted by it. He soared higher and higher until he lost sight of his chicken friends, and they lost sight of him. That day, he realized he had never been a chicken. He was just an eagle among chickens.

Are you an eagle among chickens? Get up and fly, soar! Don't let your environment or anything hinder you that you can't be what God has made you to be. A lot of lessons are to be drawn from this introductory story.

Unfortunately, many people are constraint and limited by narrow-minded and short-sighted people around them to the same level as themselves. If your friends and associates are always telling you that you cannot, it's high time you changed your circle of friends. Obviously, you're in a wrong circle. Sometimes, God must open your eyes to see that you are already what you earnestly desire to be. You are already a success. Just plan and execute. You are already loved. Stop looking for love in immorality, pre-marital, and extra-marital affairs. You are worth much more! Stop putting up with abuse and oppression. You are blessed already, stop being afraid of curses. No one can curse whom God has blessed; the scripture says if we believe in Jesus, we are blessed alongside Abraham. We are partakers of that blessing. All things are yours in Christ. Stop operating with a poverty mindset and mentality. May God open your eyes to see!

That young eagle among chickens saw eagles soaring, living his dream life. Did he react in envy or resentment? No. Most people would rather pull down those who are doing better than themselves instead of learning from them. You are to challenge yourself to desire something better – do not envy them. Learn from them and move up your ladder of success.

The Majesty of the Eagle

Proverbs 30:18-19a *"There are three things which are too wonderful for me, yes, four which I do not understand: the way of an eagle in the air…"*

To most people, the eagle is the most majestic of all birds. No wonder the ancient people call the eagle the bird of heaven. There is something wonderful about the way an eagle moves in the air. A writer wrote this about the eagle, *"Air is constantly in motion. It moves in great circles because of differences in pressure. It sometimes drops down in great downdrafts or huge updrafts where warm air rises at very high speeds — the air changes from hour to hour. The eagle lives in this vast sea of air. The eagle actually perceives this dynamic air movement and uses it to support itself and soar. It rises to thousands of feet in the air without the slightest effort. It doesn't have to flap its wings like most other birds."*

There are several biblical references likening the Eagles to us (Christians). Whenever God gives us a specific analogy in the Bible, we have to key into the revelation of that analogy in order to pick what He is trying to tell us so that we can interpret and fully understand what He is trying to convey to us. If we do, then we will see exactly what God is trying to tell us in reference to the actual analogy itself.

The 'Eagle analogy' is one of the most powerful biblical analogies. God comparing us to the Eagle. So why did God compare us to the eagle? And why not the Lion – the king of the jungle, or the Elephant (biggest land creature), or the Giraffe or even an Ostrich, the biggest bird. Why the Eagle? This question prompted me to research about Eagles and their personality traits to see why God compared us to them, to see if any traits were inherent in the Eagle that God wanted us to have. These are some of the traits and leadership principles the Eagle possesses that God would like to have worked into each one of us (Christians):

1. Eagles Are Master-Fliers: They can fly to heights that no other bird can. They have been seen flying as high as some airplanes fly. The Eagles depend on strong wind thermals to take them to heights that no other bird can fly to. In the same way, God wants all Christians to be master fliers like the Eagles, by learning to submit to the leadership and guidance of the Holy Spirit on a daily basis. It is the job of the Holy Spirit Himself to teach and empower us to accomplish everything that the Lord has set out for us to achieve.

2. Eagles Fly Alone and Love the Storm: They don't fly with sparrows, ravens, and other birds. Eagles flies with Eagles. They keep good company. The bible says, *"bad company corrupts good character."* Eagles also live on higher ground and fly at very high altitudes. As Christians, we are already living on higher ground, compared to the rest of the world because of our position in Christ Jesus. And we always need to keep reminding ourselves that we are living on this higher ground, as the world will always do everything it can to try and drag us down into their lower way of living. In other words, we are in the world, but not of the world. We are to keep ourselves separate from the corruption, pollution, vices, and sins of this world.

Eagles love the storm. When clouds gather, the eagle gets excited, while other birds will hide on tree branches and leaves for cover in safety against the raging storm. The Eagle uses the stormy wind (wind thermal) to lift itself higher. Once it finds the current of the storm, it uses the raging storm to lift above the clouds. This allows the eagle to glide and rest its wings.

The Bible likened the coming of the Holy Ghost at Pentecost in Acts 2:1-5 to the sound of a mighty rushing wind. Believers must allow themselves to be led and directed by the Spirit of God. We are not to struggle to achieve or be rigid in our own wisdom. As air movement is dynamic, so is the movement of the Spirit of God. As eagles allow the air to move it, so must you, as a believer, allow the Spirit to guide you always! When the Spirit is guiding all your endeavors, you will find yourself achieving and making an impact with little or no effort.

Moreover, eagles don't hide from storms. They use the power of air currents to rise over it. The worse the storm blows, the higher they soar. Allow the Holy Spirit to lift you over adversity. Face your challenges head-on, knowing that God is in control. Believe that with God on your side, you'll emerge stronger and better than you were. Know quite well that a Christian that cannot pray through cannot breakthrough. Also, bear in mind that as a Christian, we don't go around the storm, we go through the storm. We use the storms of life to rise to greater heights. Because achievers are not afraid to rise to greater heights. Achievers are not afraid of challenges, instead they relish them and use them profitably.

3. Eagle Has Two Sets of Eyes and Accurate Vision:

Amusingly Eagles have two sets of eyes. The first set is their natural eye, which they use normally. They activate the second set of eyes when they hit a strong wind thermal; this second eye then enables them to fly on the strong wind thermals without damaging their original eye. The second eye gives them a protective covering as they are navigating through the heavy tempest clouds.

Another very fascinating quality is their accurate vision; the Eagles have the ability to focus on a prey as far as 3 miles away. And no matter the obstacles, the eagle will not be distracted or shift its focus from the prey until he grabs it.

As Christians, we also have two sets of eyes. The first set is our natural eye, which we use to see the natural world in which we live in. However, we also have a second set of eyes, and that is the eyes of the Holy Spirit. As we draw closer to the Lord and begin to have a personal relationship with Him, there will be times that He will allow you to 'see' things as He sees them. You will start 'seeing' what certain Scripture verses really mean. You will begin to 'see' what the real truth is in many of the matters of your own personal life. The Bible says that the truth will set you free. But you first must see and know what that truth is before it can set you free. We all need the eyes of the Holy Spirit operating within us, so that we can see beyond the physical realm.

Just like the Eagle, God wants us to sharpen our vision and remain focused on the path of greatness, no matter the obstacles in our way.

4. Eagles Are Master Fishers and Hunters: They Feed only on fresh prey. Eagles are also considered master fishers and hunters. They are very good at locking in on their prey and swoop down on them, whether that prey be on land or in the water. Just as eagles are considered to be master hunters and fisherman, we (Christians) have been called by the Lord to be 'fishers of men' – Matthew 4:14. Just like Jesus and the apostles were at the very beginning of the New Testament. Personal evangelism within our own circle of influence is something that each and every Christian can do for the Lord, and it is something that we should always keep our radars up for – as you never know when the Holy Spirit will lead you to someone.

5. **Eagles Are Faithful and Committed:** When a female Eagle meets a male Eagle, and they want to mate, she test his commitment; she flies down to picks a twig (stick) and flies back into the air with the male Eagle in hot pursuit. Once she has reached a height high enough for her, she drops the stick and lets it fall

to the ground while she watches the male Eagle chase after the stick and catches it before it reaches the ground, then brings it back to the female Eagle. The female Eagle grabs the stick and flies to a much higher altitude and drops the stick again for the male Eagle to chase. This goes on and on with the height increasing each time until the female Eagle is assured that the male Eagle has mastered the art of picking the stick, which shows great commitment. Only then will she allow him to mate with her. What an ardent level of commitment? Just like the female Eagle we should test the commitment of the people around us. Whether in private life or business, so that we can know those we intend to go into partnership with.

Also, Eagles are very faithful to their spouse, once the male Eagle mates with their partners, they remain faithful to that female Eagle for life. In the same way, once God leads you to your spouse, He will expect you to remain loyal and faithful to that spouse forever. But in the world we live today, our society sees divorce as a normal thing, thus, high percentage (about 50%) of marriages are ending up in divorce, this is appalling. It is now a tall order for many to stay faithful to their spouses. But the truth is that God expects all of us to honor our marital vows and commitments made at the wedding altar. God takes marriage and the vows that come with it very seriously, and it is nothing to be trifled with or taken for granted once you hit a few minor speed bumps in your marriage.

The Holy Spirit is the helper and counselor. He can help heal any hurts or misgivings that may have occurred in your marriage if you will just open yourself up to Him and allow Him to work it out for you.

6. Eagles Prepare and Train Their Children:
The bible says in **Job 39:27** *"Is it at your command that the eagle mounts up and makes his nest on high?*

The nests of eagles are built in the wilderness, up in the mountain; far away from mainstream society where she can safely raise and train her children up without any external influence or harm coming to them. In an environment where they will grow to be eagles themselves.

The bible says, *"Train up a child in the way he should go: and when he is old, he will not depart from it"* – **Proverbs 22:6**. It is our responsibility to train and bring up our children in the way of the Lord. So that wherever they may be in the world, the light of Christ dwells in them, because they have been deeply rooted in the word of God and trained in the way of the Lord. But, if you allow the society to train your children for you, with all the moral decadences that has perverted the world, don't be surprised that the child will stray from the path that leads to eternity. Because that is all the world has to over them (disrespect, hate, bitterness, lust, immorality, confusing, circularity, rebellion, insensitivity to divine ordinance), and that is very detrimental to the child and the parents as well. We must endeavor to be the godly example our children follow.

And just like the Eagle, leave your comfort zone, there is no growth there!

7. Eagles Are Extremely Bold, Courageous, and Powerful: Boldness, courage and power is another distinctive attribute of the Eagle. They have been seen engaging with poisonous snakes and preying on animals twice their size and they triumph with the power in their claws and beak. We are expected to take a cue from the eagle and be fearless in whatever situation we find ourselves. Equally the eagle is the most powerful and feared bird in the sky – God wants us to be fearless to exhibit our God-given authority; *"For God has not given us a spirit of fear, but of power and of love and of a sound mind"* – **2 Timothy 1:7**. Because God the Father wants to personally raise you up to be a mighty, powerful and courageous soldier that will do great and mighty exploits in His kingdom.

Undoubtedly, the power and strength of an Eagle cannot be undermined amongst other birds. The same is with the greatest country in the world (USA). That's why the eagle is the ultimate emblem of America's strength and its vision of a nation with soaring aspiration.

8. Eagles Are Very Patient: Another interesting quality that distinguishes the Eagle from other birds is that it's a very patient bird. Documentary film about Eagles shows that when targeting their prey, they have the ability to wait patiently for over two hours, and when the right time comes, they swing into action without any inaccuracy. In the same way, we all need the patience of the eagle, especially in the type of world we now live in, with everything being done at breakneck speed and people's fuses being shortened as a result of the high stress that we are forced to live under in the name of advance technology.

Likewise, one of the nine fruits of the Holy Spirit is the fruit of patience – **Galatians 5:22-23.** Patience is indeed a virtue and we all need patience to weather the storm of this turbulent life, if we want to be great and make an impact.

9. The Eagle Renews Its Strength When It Grows Old:
Isaiah 40:31 *"But those who wait on the Lord shall renew their strength; they shall mount up with wings like eagles, they shall run and not be weary, they shall walk and not faint."*

"Those who wait on the Lord."

This means those who depend on God; they trust in Him for all things. They totally surrendered to Him, to His plan, His will and purposes. They have submitted all to Him. He is not only their God, but He is also their Father and Friend. These people are not running ahead of God; they seek His face. They await His direction and guidance; they yield to the nudging of His Spirit. They are obedient even in the face of adversity. These are those who wait on the Lord.

"...will renew their strength."

The word 'renew' implies a wearing away, a waxing old of something. What has not run out or run down doesn't need renewal. Their strength, being renewed, implies that they might sometimes run out of strength. Life is not a bed of roses. Sometimes there are depressing times when it seems hopeless. Sometimes the will to go on is not just there. Eagles sometimes experience this season. They become depressed and lonely. They stay in the dark places, will not hunt, will not clean their feathers, and their oil glands dry up.

Moreover, when they grow old and weary, their feathers become weak and cannot fly as high as it should. Faced with this frail and fragility, the Eagle retires to an isolated place far away in the mountains. While there, it plucks out all the weak feathers on its body and breaks its beak and claws by smashing them against the rocks until it's completely bared – what a very bloody and painful process. At such times, the other eagles who are still strong would go hunting and bring food for it until it grows new feathers, new beaks and claws, then it comes out flying higher than before.

This is the importance of having a circle of good friends and like-minded people.

Sometimes faithful Christians who trust in God may go through hard times and get pressed down, but because they depend on God and continuously look to Him for help, they are raised again. They do not go with their hard times. They do not end up as victims of circumstances; rather, they become victorious over their circumstances.

After this extensive research and discovery about the eagle and all the main qualities and traits they have, I came to the conclusion that it is not a mere coincidence that all these qualities perfectly line up with what God would like to have worked into each one of us. I believe when God says in Isaiah 40:31 that we'll *"mount up with wings like eagles,"* He meant exactly what He said, and said exactly what He meant in that verse. I believe the Lord is in the process of raising up an army of mighty eagles. As you can see, we are living in the last days as prophesied in the Bible, and God will be launching this army of eagles onto the earth in an effort to get as many people saved and on that rapture train as He possibly can before the end finally comes.

Lastly, my question to you is this? **Do you want to an Eagle Christian or a Chicken Christian?** Because chickens keep their eyes on things of this world; they never lift their head to see Him who is above. The chicken will eat dead things and unspeakable things and they are never free to fly to do great exploit. While the mighty Eagle is the most powerful and feared bird in the skies. When we see an eagle in flight, soaring on invisible air currents, we can be reminded that the Creator who supplies the eagle's strength will also strengthen us and renew us to make a great impact in life.

As you trust in God, you will give light and not burn out. You will flow to people and not run out. You will do much and not die off. You will not dry up because God is your source. You will be able to achieve much with great impact. Let God be your source, and you will not fail, fall, or falter. You will never fade away as you make God your source.

Follow the path of eagle!

CHAPTER 9

Stay on The Right Path To Make Impact

Psalms 16:11 *"You make known to me the path of life; in your presence there is fullness of joy; at your right hand are pleasures forevermore.*

I want you to take an assessment of where you are on the path of life. Does this biblical passage testify to your life, or do you find these godly promises not springing forth or manifesting in your life? Perhaps, it could be that you made few mistakes here and there, took wrong distracted turns that diverted the trajectory of your life, or perhaps your feet is still firm on the path of life, where righteousness, peace and joy in the Holy Spirit abides. The Bible makes it clear that you should *"Watch the path of your feet and all your ways will be established"* – **Proverbs 4:26**

Matthew 7:13-14 *"Enter by the narrow gate; for wide is the gate and broad is the way that leads to destruction, and there are* *many who go in by it. "Because narrow is the gate and difficult is the way which leads to life, and there are few who find it.*

According to this bible passage, the main reason most people are at the backward side of life is basically because of the momentous choice they made at one point in the journey of their life. This scripture further emphasizes that there are times you come to a decision-making pathway of life, where one path is very narrow (unpleasant to follow), and the other is broad and attractive to follow.

The book of **Galatians 5:16-17** says, *"walk in the Spirit, and you shall not fulfill the lust of the flesh". "For the flesh lusts against the Spirit, and the Spirit against the flesh; and these are contrary to one another, so that you do not do the things that you wish."*

The path of the flesh (carnal) looks quite attractive, popular and enticing. It's a path that logically makes the best sense to our carnal viewpoints. But as you journey on that path, it suddenly becomes a consuming snare of misery. We are often tempted to take this path basically because it offers the most minimal resistance, it's broader, easier to maneuver and it glitters falsely to attract unsuspecting victims. But in the real sense, it's all vanity and worthlessness as it leads nowhere but eternal damnation. But, factually, our spirit (inner man) yarns for the narrow path, because we know within us that it's the right path, but we ignore our inner spirit because of the gratification and weakness of the flesh that suppresses us to turn the other way that leads nowhere. The bible confirms this assertion that *"... the spirit is willing, but the flesh is weak"* – **Matthew 26:41b**

Then, how do you make the right choice that leads to eternal redemption and everlasting life? Apparently, it is your commitment, dedication and devotion to God that will make you turn to the right direction at the junction-path of life. As the bible passage above stipulates, the choice is either the broader way that seems glittering, enticing and popular which attracts lots of traffic but eventually ends up in doom, or the narrow path, which is a difficult, commitment demanding path which eventually leads to eternal salvation, fruitfulness, and a path of impact.

Moreover, to follow the path that will influence and impact the world, takes a total reliance, and a complete trust in God. If your purpose and will does not align with the purpose and will of God for you, there is no way you can be on the path that fulfills destiny, not to talk of making an impact in the world or in the lives of others. Total submission to God's will, guidance and direction is the key to unlocking your path to greatness and destiny manifestation. God reiterated this promise in Isaiah 42:16 *"I will lead the blind by ways they have not known, along unfamiliar paths I will guide them; I will turn the darkness into light before them and make the rough places smooth. These are the things I will do; I will not forsake them."*

But, the issue with some folks is that they tend to be like sheep, having the tendency to go astray and lose focus on the path that dependably directs us to the path of God's abundant grace and mercy. It's only when we stay true to our faith and committed to the path that God is leading us, that's when we can continuously enjoy all the promises God stipulated in the scriptures above.

The Path You Choose Matters – The Right or Wrong Path:

When I look at the world we live in today as Christians, I could possibly divide the people into two broad categories:

First, there are those who approach the race of their life with enthusiasm, strong passion, and great resilience. They never give up or change course on the path God has placed them to make impact. They become fruitful in their pursuit of greatness. They walk confidently in the victory that the Lord purchased on the cross at Calvary, knowing fully well that nothing can debar or detour them from this path of victory.

The second group, on the other hand, are those who are languishing on the broad path of life that leads nowhere but regret, ruin and disappointment. They are worn-out, weary, heavy laden, bitter, depressed and disillusioned. They look not unto God but continue steadfastly in sin. They pray without faith and often chase after the vain things of this world without regard for eternity. They have no passion or thirst for the word of God; thereby, have little or no success to show for their carnal endeavors.

The difference between these two groups of people is the choice of the path each chose to follow. The Bible counsels us to ponder on the path we choose – **Proverbs 4:26** *"Ponder the path of your feet and let all your ways be established"*. It's obvious that the path you consciously or unconsciously choose will determine if you will fulfil destiny or not.

Genesis 13:10 *"And Lot lifted his eyes and saw all the plain of Jordan, that it was well watered everywhere (before the LORD destroyed Sodom and Gomorrah) like the garden of the LORD, like the land of Egypt as you go toward Zoar."*

In this scripture, Lot was seeing with his carnal eyes and fleshly viewpoint and thus overlooked God's original purpose for his life, his wrong and fleshly choice ensnared him for disaster. This path led Lot into a sinful nation of Sodom and Gomorrah, it took the timely intervention of Abraham (his uncle) to rescue him out. At the end of the day Lot has no good testimony to show for the path he chose, rather he was overwhelmed with disaster, calamities and misfortunes. The bible says *"There is a way which seems right to a man, but its end is the way of death"* – **Proverbs 14:12.**

More so, to stay on the right path, you must follow the path that leads to the cross. And for you to continually stay on this right path, you must constantly keep your eyes on Christ and His Purpose. Because Jesus purposed it for you to make impact here on earth and further receive the crown of glory in heaven and be seated with Him at the right-hand side of the Father – Colossians 3:1-2 *"If then you were raised with Christ, seek those things which are above, where Christ is, sitting at the right hand of God. Set your mind on things above, not on things on the earth."*

Briefly, let me draw comparison from this story of a hunting dog I read online.

"A particular hunter bought a new hunting dog. He was eagerly ready to know how his new hunting dog would perform. Then he took the dog out to trail a bear. Shortly into the woods, the hunting dog picked up the track of a bear, the dog suddenly stopped, sniffed the ground, and moved in a new path. He had caught the scent of a deer that had crossed the bear's path. A few minutes later, he stopped again, this time smelling a rabbit that had crossed the path of the deer. And the dog kept changing

course until the breathless man (hunter) caught up with his dog, only to find it barking triumphantly down the hole of a field mouse."

Sometimes we are like that hunting dog. We often begin highly determined with great zeal, making Jesus first in our lives and everything we do. But sooner than later, we succumb to the untold pressure the world places on us, and thereby, turn our attention to other lesser pursuits, that will eventually stray us from the original path. The psalmist rightly counsels us to turn away our eyes from looking at worthless things so that God will revive us in His way – Psalms 119:37.

At this point, the truth you need to understand is that you need the wisdom of God to stay on the right path, as you now know that remaining on the right path requires continuous commitment, dedication, seeking God's guidance and direction in all your endeavors. With this in mind, you will no doubt make impact that will be greatly felt.

God says, *"I have directed you in the way of wisdom; I have led you in upright paths"* – Proverbs 4:11. So therefore, I indulge you to stay on the right path and begin to make an impact!

CHAPTER 10

Follow the Path of Consistent Faith

It's very obvious that we all desire to be on the right path in our lives, but life always brings us to several crossroads of decisions that often demand our choice to either rely on self or persist with unwavering faith in God. Besides, the only way to make impact towards destiny fulfilment, is by following the path of consistent faith.

"If you wait for perfect conditions, you will never get anything done." – Ecclesiastes 11:4. From this scripture, it's obvious that God wants us to always take timely decisions that are based on His prophetic directives, instead of getting lazily tied down in our comfort zone waiting for the perfect time that's not quite feasible. God wants us to follow His living revelations, not just

waiting for perfect conditions spawn out of fear and lack of faith.

God don't often show us the full image or foreknowledge of where He's taking us, but wants us to completely trust Him with unshaking faith. This is how God operates the path of faith – believing without seeing, which is exactly what faith is all about, and that's our core value also as believers. Faith is a physical reaction and responses to a spiritual reality. The bible put this in proper perspective that *"faith is the substance of things hoped for, the evidence of things not seen"* – Hebrew 11:1. Simply put, faith is what you cannot see, but deeply belief and convinced in your soul it's real. It's indeed the understanding that there is a path that is purposed for you beyond our logical reasoning. However, the fundamental truth is that at one point or the other we must decide whether to rely on our fear or faith. Fear will always make you indecisive, procrastinate, and keeps telling you to trade safely and wait for the coast to clear, but faith on the other hand will tell you to trust God consistently, because, He is in control and He knows and has the best plan for you.

Frankly speaking, it's hard to be a person of faith. Because faith in God doesn't mean falling into a perfect life. It does not mean a pain or hurt free path, or an easy way. *But the assurance is that anything life brings your* way, you can be rest assured that you have a God who will not forsake you in all the trials of life.

Let me tell you one of my favorite stories: 'the forty martyrs of Sebaste.' I believe this story will no doubt inspire you to persist in the path of faith no matter what the obstacle may be, **even in a matter of life and death:**

> "The forty martyrs of Sebaste or the Holy Forty, these forty soldiers, all Christians, were members of the famous Twelfth Legion of Rome's Imperial Army. These forty soldiers were stationed in Sebaste, a remote Armenian town. While they were brave soldiers, they were also devoted Christians, who had openly confessed their faith in Christ. One day their captain told them Emperor Licinius had sent out an edict that all soldiers were to offer sacrifice to the pagan gods. These courageous Christians replied, **'You can have our armor and even our bodies, but our hearts allegiance belongs to Jesus Christ.'** Upon hearing this in Rome, the infuriated Emperor planned a cruel death for them. It was midwinter of A.D. 320, it was bitterly cold in Sebaste at that time of the year and the captain had them marched onto a nearby frozen lake looking across the waters at the glowing fires of the pagans god – where they could go and be spared from death, if they would renounce Jesus Christ. Still they refused! He stripped them of their clothes and gave them the choice to either freeze to death or renounce Jesus Christ as their Lord and

Savior. Still they refused to renounce Jesus! Instead, throughout the night, these men huddled together singing their victory song, **'Forty martyrs for Christ.'** *As death approached, a band of angels came down from heaven and placed crowns on the heads of these dying saints. One by one the frozen temperature took its toll and that freezing night saw thirty-nine of them fall to their icy graves. At last there was only one man left. He lost courage and stumbled to the shore, where he renounced Christ. One of the officers guarding them had been watching all this. Unknown to the others, he had secretly come to believe in Christ. When he saw this last man break rank, he walked out onto the ice, threw off his clothes, replaced the man who had renounced Jesus and he confessed his faith in Christ and died alongside these Christian warriors. When the sun rose the next morning, the Roman soldiers found forty men who had given all to Christ."*

This story demonstrated the power of consistent and unshakable faith in God even though these Christians martyrs all died at the end of the story. But the path of faith they followed made great impact in the whole world. As a result of their martyrdom, people were motivated and inspired by their act of faith and many people came to know Christ; many churches where built across Europe and beyond to commemorate them. As a matter of fact, the impact of their ardent faith in God is still lingering after over seventeen hundred years (1700 years) it happened. Death, in this case was a supreme test of their faith. Dying sometimes is our last and perhaps greatest opportunity to witness for Christ's glory. And sometimes the testimony of faith under trial is louder than the testimony of words.

Similarly, the story of Daniel in the bible – Daniel 6:1-28, correlate the same pattern of unwavering faith. Daniel lived a consistent life of faith, faced with a similar kind of trial of faith. His faith was challenged by the mighty king, with threat to be thrown in the lion's den. But he persisted in faith in God against a deadly threat. Eventually, Daniel's faith had made an impact on the king of Babylon and the entire nation. Even the king came to believe and have faith in the Lord. You see, when faith is exercised truly, it transforms others to be faithful in God. Also, when faith is practiced consistently, it inspires others to come to faith and help them grow.

What we can learn from these two stories of unshakable faith in God, is that, consistency and total reliance on God pays off, whether it's ending up in a glorious exit as in the case of the forty martyrs of Sebaste or timely intervention from the lion's den in Daniel's case. Mostly it's not all about how you start or finish the race, though it's very important, but God is more interested in us running faithfully all the way. Because God is honored by the faith of His people.

Abraham is another outstanding example in the bible of someone who chose the path of faith and it led him to inherit God's blessings. He followed God with blind faith. God asked him to leave his birthplace, family and everything he grew up to know, to follow Him to an unknown promised land. The bible makes it known that, *"By faith Abraham, when called to go to a place he would later receive as his inheritance, obeyed and went, even though he did not know where he was going"* – Hebrews 11:8. We might not see or know the final destination of our journey of faith, but God knows it all. Faith is the only path to follow to prove to God that we trust and totally rely on Him. The bible rightly put it that, *"Without faith, it is impossible to please God"* – Hebrews 11:6.

More so, you don't have to be afraid of following God into the unknown because nothing is unknown to Him. The path of faith won't always feel right. Because, faith does not rely on what we feel, but on what we know. You must believe that God is always leading you for your good, because God is a rewarder of those that diligently seek Him. If you choose to live your life for Jesus, holding nothing back, He'll always lead you to the right path of destiny fulfillment. You can wisely say that following God's guidance and direction can only lead to the good path of life. But have it in mind that, the right path may not be easy along the line, but you must trust that Jesus knows where he's leading you. At the end it's worth all the energy and devotion put in.

Finally, the Apostle Paul proclaimed in the book of Hebrews that faith in God is a sign of assurance that one is destined for the future Kingdom of God which is understandably 'unseen.' And faith is the foundation for our relationship with God and everything that it implies within His purpose.

So, what path is God directing you to take? Will you say no to fear and step out in faith? What has God been putting in your heart that you know you need to do? Follow the path of consistent faith in whatever you do because it will lead you to success and an impactful life.

As you walk this journey called life, I remind you to stay close to God-your guide and enjoy the trip!

CHAPTER 11

Put Your God Given Gifts to Use

Romans 12:6 *"Having gifts that differ according to the grace given to us, let us use them..."*

As Christians, we are all endowed with gifts and talents by God and we are expected to use our gifts to glorify Him. There are possibly many area and opportunities where you can use your gifts for God! Though, gifts may vary from person to person, but the fact is that we all have gifts deposited in us by the Almighty God waiting to be used for destiny fulfilment. Some use their gifts actively or passively and some don't use their gifts at all. Some gifts are public, while some are privately – behind the scenes. Some gifts and talents are meant to be used within the church, others outside (world) and at the same time some gifts and talents are to be used for our personal prominence and fame as the bible recorded that *"A man's gift makes room for him, and brings him before great men"* – Proverbs 18:16

Our God is so good, and He surely knows how to give us (His children) good gifts that will direct us to finding and fulfilling our purpose in life. The gifts of God in our life can make us become so blessed and in turn we become a blessing to others. God who makes heaven and earth intends for us to impact the world with the wonderful gifts and talents that He has purposefully given to us.

Activate your gifts to find your purpose (Use your gifts):

James 1:17 "Every good gift and every perfect gift is from above, coming down from the Father of lights with whom there is no variation or shadow due to change."

From this bible passage we know that God's gifts are from His throne of grace. Not that we actually merited it, because it's free and unmerited. For example, God's gift of His only begotten son for the remission of our sins, was done out of genuine love. God gives gifts because that's His nature, every good gift and every perfect gift comes from Him. God gives us gifts and talents so that we can effectively impact lives for His unshared glory. In other words, our gifts are not just for our self alone, our gifts are meant to serve others, even, our Lord Jesus Christ demonstrated this throughout His earthly ministry, by being the servant – master. If you limit your gifts and talents to yourself, then you cannot affect the lives of others around you and thus it will be difficult to leave a legacy and impact that will last long.

For instance, if someone has the gift of serving or ministering, it is not to serve himself but to serve and minister to others. Likewise, if you have the gift of giving, it so that you can use your resources to uplift the gospel; invest in people (human capital development). A lot of people will not be remembered over time by the beautiful houses, cars they had, but will be remembered for the number of people they impacted and empowered to fulfil their dreams and aspiration. That is the kind of legacy and impact that will stand forever.

The reason God gives us gifts and talents in the first place is so that we can be a blessing for a noble course. The bible makes it known that *"As each one has received a gift, minister it to one another, as good stewards of the manifold grace of God"* – **1 Peter 4:10.**

Ephesians 4:11–12 "And he gave the apostles, the prophets, the evangelists, the shepherds and teachers, to equip the saints for the work of

ministry, for building up the body of Christ." There is a misconception that its only pastor or church leaders that have been gifted to do all the church work. But the scripture above points it out that they are to equip the saints for the work of ministry. However, it is the saints who build up the body of Christ. Use your gifts and talents to serve others, as we are all called to serve each other. The bible further confirms this ***"from whom the whole body, joined and held together by every joint with which it is equipped, when each part is working properly, makes the body grow so that it builds itself up in love"*** – **Ephesians 4:16.**

The question most people often ask is, what if I don't know what my gift is? That's simple! Begin serving wherever you can, in whatever capacity you can. Serve wherever there's a need. And as you serve, God will make your area of gifting clear to you and even others can confirm it. As a matter of fact, you can use your gifts and talents in different facets, even in the least possible areas you would think of. For instance, if your God given talent is in the area of entertainment like singing, dancing or playing instruments, you could be useful in the worship or drama department in your church. If your church doesn't have that department, assemble a team of other talented and gifted people to start that department in your Church. You can additionally bless people within your community with this gift by offering free performances to community centers, old people's home, schools, and homeless shelters. By so doing, you can minister to them in prayers and convey the word of God's salvation to them as well. Also, if your talent is teaching, you can be useful as a Sunday school teacher or perhaps teach a class in the children's department.

Likewise, if your gift is administrative. Your gift is the pillar of the success of any organization, because your gift can be of help to all other gifts and talents. For example, people who are gifted but don't know where and how to start, you'll use your gift to help them. Your gift is a foundational gift that helps the church and the world at large by supporting, directing and organizing for others. In a simple term, your talent is to help others get their gifts and talents up and running!

If you are gifted and talented in communication, there are diverse areas you can display your talents to the world, be it words of encouragement, motivational speaking, social media communication etc., all you need is to develop a solid content and then find a platform to disseminate your talents to the world. There are numerous platforms that you can use and it's much easier now with the proliferation of the internet and other social media platforms like, YouTube, Facebook, Instagram, Twitter and so on. You can showcase your talents to the whole world in a twinkle of an eye – the world is now a global village where information travels at unimaginable speed from one part of the world to another. Use your gift to personally showcase your talent and communicate the Gospel and draw people to Christ, which is the ultimate goal and the main reason for the gifts in the first place.

Lastly, if you can serve in any capacity in the church, great! But you can also use your gifts and talents to serve in many ways outside the church: You can give encouraging words to comfort people in grief. You can minster to the sick through prayer. If you are financially buoyant, you can support the church and needy. You can serve in a pro-life or campus ministry. Input Business ideas. Use your professional sport, and entrainment skills to serve. Every tiny act of service is pleasing to God. Remember Jesus said if you give someone a drink of water in His name, you won't lose your reward – Matthew 10:42.

The bible also recorded that *"there are different kinds of gifts, but the same Spirit distributes them. There are different kinds of service, but the same Lord. There are different kinds of working, but in all of them and in everyone it is the same God at work"* – 1 Corinthians 12:4-6. So, whatever your gifts and talents are use them to glorify God and not for self-glorification.

Finally, as you serve faithfully, God will make your gifts clear and once you know your gifts you will easily find your purpose in life and once you find your purpose, you would be on the path to impact the world tremendously.

Put your God given gifts to use!

CHAPTER 12

Don't Stop! You Are Making A Mark Already

The story I am about to share saddens me slightly but fires me up whenever I remember it. There was this old man who was given to evangelism. He would stand at the same spot everyday handing tracts to people. He did this for many years without noticing any fruit of his labor. After a while, discouragement crept into his heart, and he began to listen to the whispers of the enemy. The enemy told him, "You've been doing this for a long while now, and nobody has changed. Why continue? You are just wasting your time!" This satanic thought became a stronghold in his heart, and he harkened to this evil thought that has taken over his mind, then he stopped evangelizing completely. After a few months, he was passing by that same spot. Guess what he saw? A young man stood where he used to stand precisely, doing what he used to do! Wow! Was he replaced so fast? He decided to go nearer and see for himself.

When he got closer, the young man who replaced him, exclaimed with surprise and embraced him. The young man said, "You may not know me, sir, but I used to be a criminal, and one day you gave me a tract here. I read it, believed the gospel, and was converted. When I noticed you no longer come here, I assumed you had passed on to be with the Lord, so I decided to continue the work, so that the work may not stop." The old man was tearful. He had allowed discouragement to stop him and was regarded dead while still alive. He didn't pass on into glory; he passed away into discouragement – sponsored by lack of perseverance! The old man gave up at the edge of his breakthrough, he forgot the word of God that said *"I come quickly; and my reward is with me, to give every man according as his work shall be"* – Revelation 22:12.

Revelations 3:11 *"I am coming soon. Hold on to what you have, so that no one will take your crown."*

This was the message of Jesus to the church of Philadelphia. The Lord knew they were barely holding on, he knew their strength was little, and it was tempting for them to stop. He was encouraging them to hold on. He has plans for them. There is a crown he is reserving for them, but they were to endure to the end so that they can have it.

Many people are like the old man in the story above, they give up on the eve of their breakthrough. They give up at the eleventh hour. His labor of many years has gone down the drain. And another man has taken his place. Have you ever been ready just to give up at any time, particularly when nothing seems to be going right in your business, job, studies or in your ministerial calling? Perhaps you are ready to give up because you've had enough. Today I want you to take a cue from Timothy – Apostle Paul's spiritual son. Pastor Timothy was apparently upset about how things are going in Ephesus too. Apostle Paul must strengthen his hand with a lot of encouragement in his second epistle to Timothy.

Likewise, I encourage and motivate you, don't stop! Don't stop attempting the seemingly impossible. You are almost there. Before you know it, you will be at the top, don't stop climbing. Don't close down your business. Don't give up on your child. Don't neglect or abandon your problematic marriage. Don't commit suicide. Keep forging ahead, help is on the way. Your breakthrough is so near, I can feel it! Don't allow the devil to feed you with his lies and wrong notions. One thing you should know about the devil is this; there is no truth with him – the scripture says he is the father of lies. Believe the exact opposite of whatever he says to you. If he tells you it is over, that's a lie, know that you have a new beginning. If he says nobody cares, believe me, many people care, God, Himself does. If he says you are failing, know that you are succeeding even if you cannot see it yet.

Keep holding on! It won't take long anymore. Your time will come before you realize it. God's appointed time is the right time, and that time is closer than you think. If you are experiencing a lot of disappointment and challenges, know for a fact that you are on the right path and you are doing something right that why Satan is discouraging you, at that point the best thing to do is to forge ahead and never give up and don't stop. The bible makes it clear that *"...it is those who endures to the end shall be saved"* – Matthew 24:13.

Besides, if you have set your feet on the path of making an impact, don't stop. You are making an impact already. Somebody somewhere is looking at you, drawing courage from your courage, taking after your lifestyle. Continue to follow the example of Christ as others emulate you. Apostle Paul said, "imitate me as I imitate Christ." Always be the first bible people get to read! A certain great man of God once shared how he learned to pray. He said as a new Christian, he didn't know how to pray. He used to wonder what people say in prayers. He then spotted one brother in the church whom he noticed was prayerful, and he decided to sit close to the brother, continually listening to his prayers. He did this and was repeating words after the brother, he did this until he learned how to pray. We don't know the name of this brother. The brother probably never knew how he has contributed to the spiritual life of this great man of God, how he had mentored him unaware. Let this encourage you. You are probably mentoring a lot of people unknown to you. Don't be discouraged and don't stop.

A Word for Those Who Are Hesitating: You Too Can Make Impact

Perhaps you are at the valley of decision, wondering what you can do, belittling the little that you have or perhaps you are unaware to the great potentials that lies within you. Many people have allowed their situations to give them a disproportionate perception of themselves. I tell you this; you can make an impact. You don't have to be big or rich or educated or mightily spiritual before you can make an impact. All you need is a good heart. Everyone can make an impact, and that includes you! Remember God's promise in the book of Job chapter eight verse seven that *"Though your beginning was small, yet your latter end would increase abundantly."* That promise still stands because God never fails you. Believe it and start making an impact.

Two Unlikely People Who Made Great Impact

John 6:5-14 *"Then Jesus lifted up His eyes, and seeing a great multitude coming toward Him, He said to Philip, "Where shall we buy bread, that these may eat?" But this He said to test him, for He Himself knew what He would do. Philip answered Him, "Two hundred denarii worth of bread is not sufficient for them, that every one of them may have a little." One of His disciples, Andrew, Simon Peter's brother, said to Him, "There is a lad here who has five barley loaves and two small fish, but what are they among so many? "And Jesus took the loaves, and when He had given thanks, He distributed them to the disciples, and the disciples to those sitting down; and likewise of the fish, as much as they wanted. So, when they were filled, He said to His disciples, "Gather up the fragments that remain, so that nothing is lost." Therefore, they gathered them up, and filled twelve baskets with the fragments of the five barley loaves which were left over by those who had eaten. Then those men, when they had seen the sign that Jesus did, said, "This is truly the Prophet who is to come into the world."*

Look at how a great need in the ministry of Jesus was met by the timely intervention of the five bread and two fishes of that young boy. The great lesson from this bible passage is that your little resources can be used to bring great glory to God. There were people there who believed in Jesus because of this miracle. How was the miracle possible? A little boy released the little he had.

Another good example is when God said to Moses, "Raise your staff and stretch out your hand over the sea to divide the waters so that the Israelites can go through the sea on dry ground." Notice that the only thing that Moses had was his faith in God and a stick in his hand. God can certainly use what you have no matter how little or insignificant they are.

What has God given or deposited in you to move you and lead others to their destiny? Perhaps it's a gift, talent or skill, that you deemed insignificant, that will lead to a path of destiny fulfilment for others. It doesn't matter what it is but use it for the Glory of the Lord.

Perhaps it's a spiritual gift such as preaching or teaching, intercession or the spiritual gift of encouraging others. Whatever it might be, put it to use in the Kingdom of God for His glory and honor. It will not only lift you higher but lift others too. So therefore, put your faith in Jesus and what He accomplished. His work not yours!

2 Kings 5:1-3, 14-15 *"Now Naaman, commander of the army of the king of Syria, was a great and honorable man in the eyes of his master, because by him the Lord had given victory to Syria. He was also a mighty man of valor, but a leper. And the Syrians had gone out on raids and had brought back captive a young girl from the land of Israel. She waited on Naaman's wife. Then she said to her mistress, "If only my master were with the prophet who is in Samaria! For he would heal him of his leprosy."*

So he went down and dipped seven times in the Jordan, according to the saying of the man of God; and his flesh was restored like the flesh of a little child, and he was clean. And he returned to the man of God, he and all his aides, and came and stood before him; and he said, "Indeed, now I know that there is no God in all the earth, except in Israel; now therefore, please take a gift from your servant."

Can you imagine what impact a little slave girl made? What does a slave girl have to offer her master? But, see how the knowledge of God and His prophet, which she shared, changed the life of her master forever! That little knowledge you have, which you are belittling, might be life-changing, lifesaving for someone. Just open your mouth and share it. If this little slave girl can make an impact and make an eternal memorial for herself, you can too! You can make an impact. I urge you to set yourself free from the shackles of limitations and constraint because that is the only thing limiting you. You can make an impact. Just do it!

Be an Elephant:

Let me tell you a fictitious story I once read, the story is about an elephant and a dog that became pregnant at the same time. Three months down the line the dog gave birth to six puppies. Six months later the dog became pregnant again, and nine months on, it gave birth to another dozen puppies, the pattern continued. On the eighteenth months, the dog approached the elephant questioning "are you sure that you are pregnant? We became pregnant on the same day; I have given birth three times to a dozen puppies and they are now grown to become big dogs, yet you are still pregnant. What is going on?" 'The elephant replied, there is something I want you to understand, what I am carrying is not a puppy but an Elephant. I only give birth to one in two years, when my baby hits the ground, the earth feels its impact. When my baby crosses the road, human beings stop and watch in admiration, what I'm carrying draws attention, what I'm carrying is mighty and great.'

The moral of this story is that you should never lose faith when you see others succeeding or being blessed. The truth is that we all make different types of impact– impact differs from impact. Some make impacts within a small sphere while others make impacts that will be felt perpetually – everlasting impacts. Don't be envious of others, if you haven't received your own blessings, don't despair your days of little beginning. Because just like the elephant in the story, what you are carrying is being processed, prepared and packaged for greater impact. Always confess and say to yourself 'my time is coming, and when it hits the surface of the earth people shall yield in admiration and my generation will know that I came.'

Therefore, keep trying. Don't stop and don't quit. Winners don't quit, and quitters don't win.

God will never be able to do anything through your life if you quit. Never stop trying and never try stopping. Be an Elephant that makes a great impact!

CHAPTER 13

Mistakes You Should Never Make

The following is a summary of what you should never do. If you would be a person of impact, never make these mistakes. It is written using the ABCD acronyms as a mnemonic:

In your journey to making an impact, remember never to:

- **A – Abuse your privileges:** Don't overuse your opportunities. Don't oppress people because you are above them. Be careful how you treat people on your way up. You might meet them on your way down.

- **B – Blame others for your error:** Learn to take responsibility for your action. Do not always be playing the blame game or passing the baton of blame to someone else. You won't go far this way.

- **C – Compare yourself with others:** This is very unwise. You are unique. Your experiences are uniquely yours. Comparing yourself with others will make you lose focus.

- **D – Deny the truth:** Always embrace the truth even if it is bitter. That way, you will grow fast.

- **E – Envy others:** Stop envying others. We all have different purposes. Somebody somewhere is envying you too.

- **F – Fail to learn from failure:** Failure is feedback. Don't stay down. Learn your lesson and move on.

- **G – Give up:** If you give up, you can't progress, so don't give up. Help is on the way.

- **H – Hoard or hide knowledge:** Share the little you know with others. A river that doesn't flow out will stink.

- **I – Ignore the less privileged:** Help as many as you can. You were helped to help others. It's in helping people that you make the most impact.

- **J – Justify wrong:** Never justify what is wrong. Maintain integrity.

- **K – Keep quiet when you should talk:** Speak up when you should. Be courageous to stand for what is right.

- **L – Load your mind with guilt or negative thoughts:** If you load your mind with negatives, you will forever have negative experiences. As a man thinks, so is he.

- **M – Marry for the wrong reasons:** Marriage is important. Marriage can make or mar your future. Marry right and marry for the right reasons.

- **N – Neglect your duties:** No matter how insignificant your assignment is, do it well. If you are unfaithful in little, you won't be trusted with much.

- **O – Open your heart to wrong things:** Never allow what is wrong to gain your attention or affection. Guard your heart with all diligence.

- **P – Pay good with evil:** Do not be ungrateful. Do not bite the hands that feed you.

- **Q – Quench the Spirit:** Allow the Spirit to guide you always. He is your true teacher and helper. You are nothing without Him.

- **R – Repay evil with evil:** Vengeance is the Lord's. Never seek to take your own pound of flesh.

- **S – Slander anyone:** Do not whisper evil about anyone else. Let no untruth depart from your lips about someone else.

- **T – Tolerate evil:** Tolerance of evil is evil. Conquer evil with good.

- **U – Unite with wrongdoers:** Do not let trying to be acceptable to others make you join yourself with wrong-doers. Do not be partakers of other men's iniquity.

- **V – Victimize people:** Don't oppress anybody. Don't be wicked.

- **X – Xerox evil:** (Xerox is a photocopy machine) so, do not copy what is evil, no matter how popular it is to do so. Do not follow multitudes to do evil.

- **Y – Yarn tales:** Don't go about telling stories about people. Don't be a talebearer, gossiper, backbiter, slanderer. That's too low for you to stoop to. You are too busy making a positive impact!

- **Z – Zero your mind:** Never be devoid of ambition. Do not ever grow complacent. Don't ever let there be a time when you have no aspiration, no achievement to look forward to.

Conclusion

I once heard a fictitious story that best communicates what I want to say here. Here is the story. Satan had a conference in hell. It was tagged, "Getting many people to hell." It was a strategic conference where all his ministers (demons – falling angels) were enjoined to table their strategies towards achieving the aim described by the theme of the conference. Each had different things to say.

"I will go and tell them that there is no God." The foul spirit of atheism said.

"No, your success will be minimal. There are preachers and others that will be so convincing that they will disprove you." Satan waved him aside.
All others came, but they were all rejected by Satan. He wanted something that will work on a land-sliding scale.

Then a tiny, frail demonic spirit stepped out. "I can do it." It whispered in a barely audible voice, almost unnoticeable but with super confidence that got everyone at the meeting staring at him.

"Yes? Tell us how."

"I will allow them to go to church and conferences." It said.

"I will also allow them to read good books and spiritual materials." It continued.

"I will even let them pray hard…" Someone chuckled. Another demon laughed and said 'this is unbelievable. How can this work?

"Will you stop interrupting?" Lucifer roared at them.

The tiny demon continued "But when it comes to the time to make a decision or take action, I will tell them to wait, to think more, to be careful. I will suggest a lot of excuses into their minds…"

"My strategy is to debar them from deciding on whatsoever will do them good or change them for better."

All of hell broke into applause. They had found a strategy to keep humanity in perpetual bondage – indecision, inaction, procrastination. These are your enemies.

Luke 11:27-28 *"And it happened, as He spoke these things, that a certain woman from the crowd raised her voice and said to Him, "Blessed is the womb that bore You, and the breasts which nursed You!" But He said, "More than that, blessed are those who hear the word of God and keep it!"*

Jesus once gave a compelling sermon. Authoritative, divinely inspired, smooth, and eloquent; a woman who was present and listened to Jesus while speaking was so impressed. She said, "blessed is the womb that bore you and the breasts you sucked!"
Jesus gave her a very instructive response. He said, "more than that, blessed rather are those who hear and keep it....! It's okay to read this through and be impressed. It's okay to feel fired up. But it is best to decide and take action.

These days many people hear the word of God and appreciate what they heard. While it is good to appreciate it, the best is to keep it in your heart and apply it.

James 1:22-25 *"Anyone who listens to the word but does not do what it says is like someone who looks at his face in a mirror* [24] *and, after looking at himself, goes away and* *immediately forgets what he looks like.* ²⁵ *But whoever looks intently into the perfect law that gives freedom and continues in it—not forgetting what they have heard, but doing it—they will be blessed in what they do".*

Do not be like that man in this bible passage, who checked his reflection in the mirror, made no effort to make changes to look better, and just went on his way remaining the same.

Take decisions on what you've read and begin to make an impact! Remember, it all starts with salvation. Submit to grace teaching, be an eagle – ride your storms, and don't belittle yourself. You can equally make an impact just avoid all the mistakes that most people make.

Go on and make impacts! And let your generation yet unborn know that you came!

First Action and Step to Take

Dear friend, I want you to know that you are not reading this book by mistake, it is divinely orchestrated by the Holy spirit and today is the day of your salvation, please do not procrastinate your salvation, tomorrow might be too late, the bible says that *"In an acceptable time I have heard you, And in the day of salvation I have helped you. "Behold, now is the accepted time; behold, now is the day of salvation"* – **2 Corinthians 6:2.**

Jesus Christ advised us in the Gospel of **Matthew 6:33** to seek first his kingdom of God and his righteousness, and then all the good things we are looking and running after will be added unto us. This means that your salvation is of utmost important, if you are not safe there is no way you can make impact that would be everlasting as the Bible rightly put it that *"For what* *shall it profit a man, if he shall gain the whole world, and lose his own soul?* – **Mark 8:36**

I encourage and urge you to take action and take the first bold step towards making a lasting and eternal impact in your life. If you are not born again; and have not given your life to Jesus as your Lord and Savior, if you are not living under the grace of God, it will be impossible for you to make any impact that has eternal significance.

Our Lord Jesus Christ himself makes it known to us that 'He is the only way and the truth and the life, and no one come to the Father except through him – **John 14:6**. Jesus also affirmed that *"... unless one is born again, he cannot see the kingdom of God"* – **John 3:3**. God loves us so much that he gave his only begotten Son, that whosoever believes in him should not perish, but have everlasting life – John 3:16.

Once again, I implore you not to procrastinate your salvation. The bible says in **Hebrews 3:15** *"...Today, if you hear his voice, do not harden your hearts as you did in the rebellion."*

Therefore, if you have decided to leave a meaningful and impactful life, **please take this step of salvation by faith:**

1. Acknowledge in your heart that Jesus is Lord.
2. Confess with your mouth that Jesus is Lord: **Romans 10:9** *"that if you confess with your mouth the Lord Jesus and believe in your heart that God has raised Him from the dead, you will be saved."*
3. Believe that Jesus died for your sins and was raised three days later, ascended into heaven and will return to judge the world.
4. Repent of your sins.

Say this simple prayer of salvation out loud with faith:

"Dear God, I want to be a part of your family. You said in Your Word that if I acknowledge that You raised Jesus from the dead, and I accept Him as my Lord and personal Savior, I would be saved. So God, I now say that I believe You raised Jesus from the dead and that He is alive. I accept Him now as my personal Lord and Savior. I accept my salvation from sin right now.

I am now saved. Jesus is my Lord. Jesus is my Savior. Thank you, Father God, for forgiving me, saving me, and giving me eternal life with You. Amen!"

Congratulations! I joyfully welcome you to God's family. Now, as a way to grow closer to Him, the Bible tells us to follow up on our commitment:

1. Find a local church where you can worship God. Seek fellowship with other followers of Jesus.

2. Get baptized (Matthew 28:19-20; Acts 2:38; Mark 16:16)
3. Tell someone else about your new faith in Christ (Mark 16:15) – Evangelism.
4. Spend time with God each day. Develop a daily habit of praying and reading the word of God (Bible).
5. Ask God to increase your faith and your understanding of the His word.
6. Develop a group of believing friends to answer your questions and support you.

I congratulate you once again and I assure you that by the grace of God, you are on your way to impact the world and leave a legacy that will transcend this world!
Shalom.

References

- Anonymous writer (unknown). *Chinese Folklore: The Boy and the King.* www.facebook.com.

- Fred Needham (2019). *The Way of An Eagle in the Air.* HQL-9646, p.28-29; Christian Assemblies International.

- Horatius Bonar – Fading Away Like the Stars of the Morning. *www. hymnary.org*

- Sacred Songs for the Soul, New Dawn Publications, Spirit and Life Production, Nigeria.

- Zainab Quadri (2019). *Tai Solarin's Powerful Message on Resilience and Determination.* www.pulse.ng.

- Rick Ezell –Sermon series: Balanced Spiritual Growth: Making A Lasting Impact

References

- Wikipedia: Albert Einstein quote ""Try not to become a person of success, but rather try to become a person of value." *en.wikipedia.org/wiki/Albert Einstein*

- Wikipedia: American activist in the civil rights movement best known for her pivotal role in the Montgomery bus boycott: *en.wikipedia.org/wiki/Rosa Parks*

- Wikipedia: "Be the change you wish to see in the world." *en.wikipedia.org/wiki/Mahatma Gandhi*

- Ken Birks – The Path of Life – The Conflicting Paths Sermon outline

Scripture Index

- Matthew 2:12-23, Matthew 5:13-16, Matthew 6:8; 33, Matthew 11:28-30, Matthew 13:1-58, Matthew 24:14, Matthew 25:31-40, Matthew 28:18-20.

- Mark 10:17-31, Mark 16:15.

- Luke 5:12-15, Luke 10:25-37, Luke 12:33-34, Luke 18:27

- John 3:16, John 3:34, John 5:24, John 10:10; 27-28, John 14:26, John 15:13, John 16:13.

- Acts 10:38, Acts 16:14, Acts 17:6, Acts 18:26.

- Romans 5:8, Romans 8:1;14;28, Romans 12:1-2

Scripture index

- 1 Corinthians 1:30, 1 Corinthians 2:16, 1 Corinthians 12:1-31, 1 Corinthians 14:3, 1 Corinthians 15:33.

- 2 Corinthians 1:1-24, 2 Corinthians 5:17;21, 2 Corinthians 9:8, 2 Corinthians 11:13-15, 2 Corinthians 12:9.

- Galatians 5:1.

- Ephesians 2:8-10, Ephesians 3:20, Ephesians 4:14, Ephesians 5:1, Ephesians 6:4.

- Philippians 1:6, Philippians 2:1-30, Philippians 4:7-8; 13;19.

- Colossians 2:1-23, Colossians 4:2-18.

- 1 Timothy 6:17-19, 2 Timothy 1:5, 2 Timothy 1:7, 2 Timothy 2:15;22, 2 Timothy 3:15-15.

- Titus 1:9.

- Hebrews 4:16, Hebrews 11:1, Hebrews 12:13, Hebrews 13:5;21,

- James 1: 5-6;12;17.

- 1 Peter 2:12, 1 Peter 3:15, 1 Peter 5:7.

- 1 John 1:9, 1 John 2:27, 1 John 4:16, 1 John 5:14-15.

- Revelation 1:1

- Genesis 1:1-31

- Exodus 4:18-31, Exodus 5:1-23.

- Deuteronomy 6:1-25

- Job 33:14-15

- Psalm 1:1, Psalm 23:1-6, Psalm 32:8, Psalm 91:16, Psalm 37:1-40, Psalm 40:2, Psalm 48:14, Psalm 91:15, Psalm 94:12-14, Psalm 119.

- Proverbs 1:10; 33, Proverbs 3:5-7, Proverbs 11:14, Proverbs 16:3; 9, Proverbs 18:10, Proverbs 19:6; 21, Proverbs 22:1.

Scripture index

- Isaiah 30:21, Isaiah 41:10, Isaiah 48:17, Isaiah 55:8-9, Isaiah 58:11.

- Jeremiah 1:7-8, Jeremiah 9:23-24, Jeremiah 10:23, Jeremiah 29:11, Jeremiah 33:3.

- Joel 2:28

www.ingramcontent.com/pod-product-compliance
Lightning Source LLC
LaVergne TN
LVHW041629070426
835507LV00008B/519